Louis Pasteur

A Biography

By Albert Keim and Louis Lumet

Translated from the French by Frederic Taber Cooper

Published by Pantianos Classics

ISBN-13: 978-1-78987-468-6

First published in 1914

Contents

From the lives of men who have marked their passage with a trail of enduring light, let us piously gather, for the benefit of posterity, every detail, down to the slightest words, the slightest acts calculated to reveal the guiding principles of their great souls.

- PASTEUR

Chapter One - A Studious Boyhood

LOUIS PASTEUR is one of the glories of France, and, among them all, the one whose light shines clearest and most fertile in results. His name has radiated throughout the world, and for scientists and laymen alike it symbolises that spirit of humanity which strove to succour all the ills of his fellow men and that genius for invention which opened vast new horizons to the researches of science. His sovereignty is now undisputed, there is no nation which has not rendered him due homage, and, as his fame has widened, it has, according to his own desire, increased the moral patrimony and the intellectual force of his native land.

Louis Pasteur was descended from one of those ancient peasant families that were attached for centuries to the land they tilled, and who have given so many illustrious sons to France. In the seventeenth century his ancestors were still serfs of the soil, in Franche-Comté, and the first who arose from servitude was Louis Pasteur's great-grandfather, Claude Étienne, who, having abandoned the labour of the fields, was in the middle of the eighteenth century a tanner at Salins, and one of the bourgeoisie of that town. He came of a race distinguished for serious-mindedness and aptitude for toil, positive qualities which produced artizans solicitous of the good renown of their calling, and gifts of imagination which urged them on to raise themselves above their environment by a superior education.

Louis Pasteur's father, Jean Joseph, an orphan from early childhood, was born to Jean Henri, the third son of Claude Etienne, on the 16th of March, 1791, in the midst of the Revolution. He was reared by his grandmother, but was taken from her by the conscription in 1811, and, having been assigned to the 3rd regiment of the line, he served throughout the war in Spain in the army of the Emperor. He made a good soldier, well-disciplined and intelligent, and he won his first promotions slowly, through good conduct and calm courage: corporal in 1812, quartermaster in 1813, sergeant-major and Chevalier of the Legion of Honour in 1814. Returning from Spain, he was one of those who took part in that immortal campaign of France, in which Napoleon expended all the marvellous resources of his military genius to save the country from invasion, yet was powerless in the face of adverse fortune.

After the Emperor's abdication Jean Joseph Pasteur was placed on the retired list by the new government. He returned to Salins to resume his trade of tanner, and shortly afterwards he married Jeanne Etiennette Roqui, of an ancient family of humble station. The bare problem of living was a difficult one, for the bride had brought nothing to their union except her cheerfulness, her gentle disposition and her two industrious arms. Accordingly it was not long before Joseph Pasteur decided to try his luck by removing to Dole, and there he established himself in a modest little house in the Rue des Tanneurs. It was there that Louis Pasteur was born on the 27th of December, 1822.

The family continued in straitened circumstances, in spite of long and weary toil. He removed, a second time, to Marnoz, and at last made his permanent home at Arbois. The tannery was situated near a stream, the Cuisance, in the low-lying town, surrounded by picturesque slopes of country-side; and it was here in an austere dwelling, in the presence of living examples of energy and courage, and under the influence of a nature that was alternately gay and melancholy, that Louis Pasteur received his first impressions.

The little town of Arbois bears a coat of arms that might well have applied to the man who was not only a great scientist but also a benefactor of humanity: on a field *azure,* a pelican *or* plucking her breast above her young, supported on a nest *or,* with drops of blood *gules.* Its population, consisting of a few bourgeois families, and chiefly of vine-growers and artizans, are rough in manner and at the same time proud. They convey an impression of stalwart courage and rugged honesty. Joseph Pasteur numbered among them several chosen friends. Dr. Dumont, retired army surgeon; M. Bousson de Mairet, the historian of Franche-Comté; M. Romanet, the principal of the high school, and a few others besides who were frequent visitors at the tannery. Young Louis used to listen to their conversations, in which duty, industry and patriotism were exalted; and, through the direct influence of his father, he became imbued with high and noble sentiments.

While still very young he was sent to the primary school, and later to the Arbois *collège,* where he began his classical studies. As a pupil, he was rather slow, and gave no indication of brilliant qualities. He studied diligently, but without enthusiasm, and at times he would fall into long reveries, which seemed to isolate him from the outside world. When he was not attending his classes and during vacations, he was fond of playing and of roaming across country; but he avoided all brutal games, such as destroying nests and killing birds. For he suffered at the sight of any kind of suffering, whether of man or beast.

From his father, who was a reflective, opinionated, yet kind-hearted man, Louis Pasteur inherited a strong will, not yet sure of itself, but which was destined later on to become the dominant force of his life; a prudent judgment, a practical common sense, based upon experience which protected him from hasty conclusions; and, on the other hand, he derived from his mother the secret side, so to speak, of his nature: a quivering sensitiveness, a vivid imagination, an intuitive intelligence, which often revealed to him the hidden mystery of things, through swift, vast flashes of illumination: also, kindliness, love of the arts, and a taste for poetry.

It was undoubtedly in obedience to these tendencies, inherited from his mother, and which belonged rather to the emotional than to the intellectual side of his nature, that among all the subjects taught in the Arbois *collège* he showed no preference for anything but drawing up to the age of thirteen years.

Within the family circle he was regarded as an artist, and he enjoyed quite a little local fame. He used to draw crayon portraits, and that of his mother, done with a free hand in pastel, revealed a character dependent upon sincerity and truth. But the alluring, yet sometimes hazardous, fame of artists was not what Joseph Pasteur desired for his son; according to his grave conception of life, his highest ambition was to see him in the assured position of a professor. For the simple man had a great respect for the ability to teach, and there was no one whom he placed higher than those who preside over the unfolding and nurturing of young minds.

When barely sixteen years of age Louis Pasteur, who at this time was applying himself with tireless tenacity to the pursuit of his studies, was sent to Paris for the purpose of being prepared to enter the École Normale. This meant a sacrifice on the part of the family, which had been augmented to the extent of two young daughters. But it was lightened by the concessions made by the director of the *pension*, M. Darbet, a compatriot from Franche-Comté. Louis Pasteur left his beloved little town of Arbois accompanied by one of his fellow pupils, Jules Vercel, in October, 1838. But no sooner had he reached Paris than a sombre melancholy seized him. He could not forget the home circle he had left behind him; and in consequence of these memories that kept him awake throughout long nights he fell into a state of languor and ill health that rendered him unfit for any work.

"Oh! if I could only smell the odour of the tannery," he used to murmur to his compatriot, Jules Vercel, "I should be well again!"

Pasteur always retained his profound love for Arbois, and even in the days of his greatest fame he used to return there every year to pass his vacation.

The director of the *pension*, M. Darbet, fearing that the severe attack of homesickness from which his young pupil was suffering might have a disastrous effect upon his health, wrote to the father, and the latter, regardless of his business, hurried to his son, and promptly brought him back to the tannery.

After his return home Louis Pasteur seems for a while to have been in an unsettled state, happy to be back again with his family, and yet perhaps secretly ashamed of having failed in his duty by not staying in Paris. In this condition it was his emotional side which prevailed for the time being. And, while he continued to follow the courses in the *collège* at Arbois, he returned to his drawing and his pastels with passionate interest. He made numerous portraits of his friends and neighbours; and there are some that have qualities which reveal a true artistic talent: the mayor of Arbois, M. Pareau, the recorder of mortgages, M. Blondeau, some young girls, some old men, and one nun.

Meanwhile, having regained his courage, as though he had, once for all, triumphed over the weakness which had caused him to hesitate in his path,

Louis Pasteur finished his course in rhetoric triumphantly. But, since the *collège* at Arbois had no classes in philosophy, the problem was once more raised as to where he should continue, his studies. The Paris experiment had been disastrous. Accordingly, Joseph Pasteur decided to send his son to Besangon, which was quite near and which he himself visited occasionally for business reasons.

It is from this period that we may date Louis Pasteur's incredible capacity for work, which enabled him to endure unlimited fatigue, and also his grave, deep-seated, invincible strength of will which refused ever to recognise obstacles. A manly letter written to his father and cited by M. Vallery-Radot, his son-in-law, in the fine work which the latter consecrated to him, *La Vie de Pasteur*, reveals to us the frame of mind in which he pursued his course in philosophy. He had disowned his talent for drawing, and scorned the reputation of portrait painter which had followed him to Besançon; for he wrote, "None of this leads to the École Normale. I would rather stand at the head of my classes than receive ten thousand praises flung out superficially in the course of current conversation. We shall see each other on Sunday, my dear papa, for Monday, if I am not mistaken, will be the day of the fair. If we go to see M. Daunas (his professor of philosophy) we can talk to him about the École Normale. My dear sisters, I recommend to you once again to be industrious and to love each other. When once we have acquired the habit of work we can no longer live without it. Besides, work is the thing upon which everything else in this world depends. By means of knowledge we raise ourselves above everybody else....But I hope that you do not need this advice, and I am sure that every day you sacrifice many a moment to studying your grammar. Love each other as I love you, while awaiting the happy day when I shall be admitted to the École Normale" (January 26, 1840).

There we have the v/hole ambition of this young philosopher. He admired and respected his teachers, and he dreamed of nothing else than to become a professor in his turn and fulfil towards others that fine and noble duty of enlightening and training other minds. His application to his studies was rewarded. On August 29th, 1840, he successfully passed, at Besançon, his examinations for the degree of bachelor of letters. This was his first degree, but he was destined to follow it up by obtaining in later years every degree that the University has within its gift; for this incarnate spirit of innovation, this revolutionary genius, so to speak, had a deep respect for degrees and functions and titles which give an assured position in society. His examination was not especially brilliant, but he received good marks in Greek, Latin, philosophy and French composition, low marks in history and geography, and excellent ones in the sciences. His dominant qualities were already revealing themselves in this first examination. Furthermore, having passed his baccalaureate, Louis Pasteur, whom the director of the school had taken on as assistant tutor — for the tannery was far from prospering — continued to pursue special courses in mathematics.

This precise trend given to his studies, which delivered him over into the hands of science, in no way prevented him from appreciating literature and poetry. This was the reverse side of his nature, the sentimental and dreamy side, which had need of nourishment and which never was wholly effaced by any amount of abstract studies — studies of a kind that we should have expected to find most distasteful to him. Louis Pasteur loved, beyond all other books, the *Essay on the Art of Being Happy*, by Joseph Droz. He appreciated the honesty of its sentiments, the gentleness of its philosophy and the kindliness which emanated from one and all of its aphorisms. He also read *My Prisons*, by Silvio Pellico, some rather dull novels which he recommended to his sisters, and some poetry. He had a friend who shared his literary enthusiasms, Charles Chappuis, with whom he was destined throughout life to enjoy a more than brotherly intimacy, and they used to work themselves to the highest pitch of exaltation by reading together the *Meditations* of Lamartine. Poetry rested Pasteur after the strain of mathematics, and, far removed from figures and calculations, it afforded him emotions so delicate that sometimes he was moved to tears.

Nevertheless, Louis Pasteur was by no means neglecting his scientific studies and his preparation for the École Normale. He even thought for a time of applying for admission to the Polytéchnique, but he renounced this idea, in order not to scatter his efforts too widely. On August 13, 1842, he was passed, at Dijon, as Bachelor of Mathematical Sciences, with low notes in chemistry, and on the 26th of the same month, in the competitive examination for the École Normale, he obtained fifteenth place out of the twenty-two candidates who were declared eligible to take the second tests. Far from satisfied with this last result, he decided not to continue in the competition, but to devote another year to preparation, in order to make a brilliant entry into this great school which was the object of his highest ambitions.

To this end he left Besançon, and, strong of purpose, precociously mature, confident that this time he would be able to conquer the regret which he was bound to feel at being separated from the family that he loved so tenderly, he once more set his face towards Paris, at the end of his vacation in 1842, with the firm determination to fulfil his duty towards himself and towards science.

Chapter Two - A Laborious and Enthusiastic Youth

HE was at this time a young man with a grave and meditative face, but under an apparent coldness he hid an ardent and enthusiastic heart and an imagination ever on the alert. Louis Pasteur feared nothing from the dangers of Paris. His powerful strength of will protected him from pleasures which might otherwise have turned him from his path, and he was glad to realise how easily his passionate love of work enabled him to dispense with them.

On arriving at the Pension Barbet, situated in the Impasse des Feuillantines, he once more found Chappuis, the confidential friend and faithful companion of his leisure hours, and he mapped out his daily life in such a way as to extract a maximum of profit from the employment of his time. He roomed with a few comrades not far from the *Pension,* and his entire time was devoted to study. Too much of his time to suit Chappuis, who would have liked a greater proportion of amusement, and too much also, to suit his father, who was anxious about his health.

Louis Pasteur's habit was to rise in the morning at half past five, for he had to tutor certain pupils of M. Barbet from six o'clock until seven, for he had been admitted to the *Pension* on payment of only one-third of the usual fee; then he attended courses at the Lycée Saint-Louis, went to the Sorbonne to hear the lectures of the famous chemist Dumas, who afforded him many a devout thrill when he spoke loftily of science and of the vast horizons that it opens to the human eye. He returned from these inspiring lessons, trembling with emotion, burning with the desire to mark his own trail among those of his precursors, to be one of those who have raised a corner of the veil which hides nature's secrets from us. He was in such haste to learn, he felt such need of incessant work, that on the days of freedom, Thursdays and Sundays, he used to shut himself up in the libraries, and, whenever he consented to take a walk with Chappuis, it was only on the condition that they should discuss, as they walked, some question of literature or philosophy.

The young student's resources were very slender, in spite of the fact that the sympathy he had aroused in M. Barbet and the services he had rendered him had caused the latter to end by remitting the whole of the usual charge; yet he had sufficient to pay for his pleasures. At the urgent request of his father he consented to go on certain Sundays to dine at the Palais Royal, where the sum he spent was scarcely ever more than forty sous! And the crowning feature of this great treat was when Louis Pasteur allowed himself the luxury of the theatre, a thing which, by the way, occurred only four times during the whole period of his studies.

It was in 1843 that he achieved the height of his ambitions. He entered the École Normale, the fourth in a good class, and he was so eager to breathe the air of the famous edifice that he cut short his vacation and presented himself several days before the date of opening. His type of mind, which was in certain respects monastic, accommodated itself to the system of the École Normale; his courage was redoubled, and he not only assimilated all the courses given, but already began to make certain private researches. He had a natural thirst for fame, he glowed with enthusiasm when he read the lives of illustrious men, he was kindled with the ambition to imitate them; but his preference leaned towards those who were benefactors and whose discoveries were useful to humanity. His father wrote to him to economise his strength, and he replied, reassuring him, for the profound affection that he bore his family never wavered; but none the less he continued to work as hard as ever. Work, work, work was destined to be the maxim of his whole existence.

PASTEUR'S BIRTHPLACE - The house on the Rue des Tanneurs, at Dole, in which Louis Pasteur was bora, on December 27th, 1822, in a modest family of the laboring class.

While a student in the École Normale Louis Pasteur continued to give lessons at the Pension Barbet, in recognition of the generous treatment he had received at the hands of its worthy master; he also continued to attend the lectures of Dumas and followed him with absorbed attention, and to his great joy he was allowed to enter the laboratory of his instructor Barruel, who gave him much practical advice. From this time forward the general development of Louis Pasteur seems to have been completed, his genius was revealed under a double character which was destined to assure the immortality of his works: he had an unlimited audacity of ideas, his intuitive conceptions soared to the outermost boundaries of human thought, and, on the other hand, he bound himself down, in his experiments, to an extremely rigorous method that refused to take count of any fact that had not been strictly verified.

While still a student he already felt the need of proselytising; he wanted to disseminate the science which he was acquiring at the cost of so much energy. So, in addition to tutoring the pupils at the Pension Barbet, he appointed himself professor to his own family, his father and sisters. He gave them problems to solve, he expounded scientific theories for their benefit, and he infused into all this correspondence the ardour of a young apostle. If they ill understood the significance of his problems, and if the explanations which he furnished seemed too difficult to be grasped by minds that did not have the advantage of a scientific training, he would encourage them affectionately, and point out the high and noble necessity of constant effort. It was a debt of gratitude that he was gladly paying to his family, whose sacrifices had permitted him to obtain an education, and this touching role of the distinguished son and brother giving instruction from a distance to his aged father and young sisters reveals the bigness of his heart.

After three years at the École Normale Louis Pasteur passed his examinations for his degree in physical sciences in 1846; out of four candidates four were passed, among whom he stood third, with no special distinction.

What was the young graduate going to do? Had he not now realised his most cherished wish in attaining the goal towards which he had striven with so much persistence? But during these years of study his ambition had shifted and broadened. To be sure, he still wished to be a professor and teach the sciences; but through contact with the masters of science, and in the presence of the glory of their discoveries, he had become determined to distinguish himself in his turn by personal discoveries, almost as though he had a presentiment of his own high destiny. After he was graduated it was not without anxiety that he realised that he might be sent to some provincial college, far from all the instruments essential to him. He was spared this misfortune through the interest which he had been able to inspire in his teachers, Dumas, Delafosse and Balard, the last of whom took him as assistant in his laboratory.

What at this time was the object of Louis Pasteur's researches? How was he going to approach the great problems of science? It seems as though a sort of predestination marked out his scientific career. Pasteur, who was destined to arrive finally at the vaccines of hydrophobia, began with the study of crystals, and his whole career was a sort of luminous ascension, progressing, from the constitution of matter and its processes, all the way to the transformation of microbes, the infinitely small yet most redoubtable enemies of man, into curative agents.

Crystalography was then a new science, with hesitant and controverted formulas. Essential phenomena remained without explanation, and others were still undiscovered, escaping all observation and all control. In order to judge adequately of the inspired novelty of Pasteur's discoveries it is necessary to understand the state of this science at the moment when he began his work.

In 1840 the men of science had only chaotic knowledge of the molecular structure of crystals. "They knew the chemical molecule," writes M. Duclaux, the great authority who was one of Pasteur's disciples; "they knew that it is formed of an ordinarily fairly stable group of atoms, of which the number, the v/eight and the nature may usually be clearly defined. They knew, for example, that there are one atom of chlorine and one atom of sodium in sea salt, one atom of calcium, one atom of carbon and three atoms of oxygen in carbonate of lime. They had recognised that different composite molecules are ordinarily differentiated by the number and nature of their component atoms, but that nevertheless there are some which contain the same number of the same atoms without for that reason being identical, so that they were led to suspect that they differed in the arrangement of their atoms. What could be the relative disposition of these atoms, one to another, within the molecule? And what would be the resultant form of the molecule itself? All these were questions on which no one had any clear idea." [1]

Haüy, who had made a very special study of crystals, and had named their constructive molecule the *integrant molecule,* considered that this latter had no relation to the chemical molecule, and that their different groupings were produced by molecules identically the same. Mitscherlich demonstrated that this theory was not absolutely exact by replacing the atoms of calcium with atoms of magnesium in a crystallization of carbonate of lime, without altering its form. This constituted the phenomenon of isomorphism. Delafosse, a pupil of Haüy's, and one of Pasteur's professors, was destined to study the phenomenon of hemihedrism, that by which certain crystals evade the law of symmetry and possess one facet which has no corresponding one, but he was unable to find the explanation. On the other hand, Biot had for a long time been investigating the rotary power of hemihedric crystals, and he had established that certain of them could deflect polarised light to the right and others to the left. This necessitates an explanation which we will borrow from M. Duclaux:

"We all know." he writes, "that every luminous impression is the result of a vibration accomplished after the fashion of a rigid rod which, held in a vise at one of its extremities, vibrates at the other by oscillating around its position of equilibrium. Now, if at the movable extremity it has a polished button reflecting a point of light, we can make this point of light describe an ellipse, a circle or a straight line. Let us examine this last case, which is the simplest, and let us agree to give the name of *plane of polarisation* to the plane which contains the vibrating rod and the line of light described by its extremity. Let us suppose that this plane is vertical and that the point of light is moving before us in line with the hands of a clock pointing to six o'clock. So long as there is nothing but the air intervening between the point of light and our eye, the vibration will not change its direction; but there are certain transparent substances which, when traversed by it, would turn it to the position of the hands of a clock pointing to five minutes to five, if the substance passed through were of a given thickness, and to ten minutes to four if it were double that thickness. In other terms they cause the plane of polarisation to rotate to the left to an extent proportionate to their thickness. We will call substances having the power of rotation to the left *left substances.* There also exist certain *right substances,* for which, *mutatis mutandis,* the definition is the same."

Young Louis Pasteur entered upon his work in the full midst of the evolution of the science of crystalography, which led from physics towards chemistry, that was still full of unsolved problems. In pursuing the work required for the last of his university degrees he tried to reconcile those personal studies that were dictated by his individual taste with those that were to give him the high title of Doctor of Science. He initiated himself into the practical manipulation of the laboratory, he trained himself in those infinitely delicate experiments which, if they are to be profitable and fruitful, demand calmness and unremitting attention. With a profound sense of realities he recommenced, as a test of his own accuracy, the experiments of La Provostaye in tartaric acid and the tartrates, seeking above all to learn whether, by following the same procedure, he would obtain the same results.

For Louis Pasteur this was a period of intellectual fermentation, in which ideas flowed to his brain in extraordinary abundance, some of them perhaps still confused, but for the most part new and destined to open up unforeseen paths to science. On the 23d of August, 1847, he defended his theses for the doctorate, which were piously dedicated to his father and mother, the one in chemistry treating of R*esearches into the Capacity of Saturation of Arsenious Acid* and forming a *Study of the Arsenites of Potash, Soda and Ammonia,* and that in physics containing a Study of the Phenomena relating to the Rotary Polarization of Liquids. Following his defense of these theses, which won him the degree of Doctor, he took an extremely brief rest at Arbois, and it was with a sort of feverish impatience that he returned to Paris to continue his study of crystals. It was destined to continue for five years and to end by shedding light upon what had hitherto been nothing but darkness and confusion.

It is impossible to mention all the details and fluctuations of this research, for, while great flashes of inspired intuition opened up new aspects of science, he verified them by so many experiments, rigorously conducted and frequently repeated, that a detailed account would mean a bulletin of his daily toil. In proportion as he obtained results he addressed notes to the Academy of Sciences, the first dating from 1848, *Note on the Crystallization of Sulphur, Researches into the different Modes of Grouping in Sulphate of Potash, Researches in Dimorphism, Memorandum on the Relation which may exist between Crystalline Form and Chemical Composition and on the cause of Rotary Polarization.*

These austere labours, this life of the laboratory, which kept his mind constantly occupied and concentrated on problems difficult of solution, nevertheless in no wise isolated him from the vital interests of the French nation. In common with all other young students, he had thrilled at the proclamation of the Republic in 1848, and it was with enthusiasm that he greeted the words, "Liberty, Equality, Fraternity." Light of purse though he was, our young savant gave to his country his entire savings, one hundred and fifty francs, and he was delighted to serve in the national guard. It was a duty which he joyfully performed on behalf of his native land, for under all circumstances Pasteur was a man who did his duty.

A cruel bereavement was destined shortly afterwards to interrupt his activities during several months. His mother died suddenly, in May, 1848, and it is easy to conceive how keen his grief was, since we know what a profound affection he cherished for his family, which, equally with science, held first place in his thoughts. For long weeks he found himself incapable of accomplishing any work, yet nevertheless he continued the course of his studies, so keen was his passion for scientific research.

Meanwhile his communications to the Academy of Science had attracted the attention of the learned world to his work. Its full value and originality were recognised and the highest expectations were held regarding his further researches. Pasteur, who in a vague way was already conscious of his genius, regarded them as no more than a schoolboy's clever essays, but in his study of the tartrates and paratartrates he was destined to distinguish himself in a marvellous manner. Without entering into a minute explanation of these questions, it should be understood that Mitscherlich, who had made some remarkable experiments with crystals, had proved that tartrates and paratartrates were the same identical salts, excepting that the former acted upon polarised light and possessed a rotary power, while the latter remained without action. It is at this precise point that we are forced to admire the inspired intuition of Pasteur, who, starting from a preconceived idea, proved experimentally that it was correct. Why was there this difference, he asked himself, between salts which appeared to be identical? Undoubtedly it was due to a difference in their composition which had an influence upon their external aspect, a difference which had not yet been observed. And this difference he discovered by a searching examination of these crystals. The tartrates had one hemihedric facet — were *manchots*, one-armed, to borrow M. Duclaux's vivid simile — while the paratartrates obeyed the law of symmetry in regard to their facets. The rotary power was directly related to the dissymmetry of the molecular structure. This first discovery was followed by a second, which was in a way a consequence of it and which revolutionised all the hitherto acquired knowledge of molecular composition. Pasteur resolved to find out why the paratartrates did not deflect light; he analysed them anew, at great length, and he perceived that the double paratartrates of sodium and ammonia, like those of sodium and potassium, had hemihedric crystals, but that the ones were left-handed and the others right-handed. This seemed to contradict his first discovery, and it was at this point in his labours that his decisive experiment took place. "In spite of much that was unexpected in this result," he said, "I none the less continued to follow up my idea. I carefully separated out the right-hand hemihedric crystals and the left-hand hemihedric crystals, and I observed separately the effect of their solutions in the polarising apparatus. I then saw, with no less surprise than delight, that the right-hand hemihedral crystals deflected the plane of polarisation to the right, and the left-hand hemihedral crystals deflected to the left; and, when I took an equal weight of each kind of these crystals, the mixed solution was neutral in its effect on polarised light, through the neutralisation of the two individual deflections that were equal and in opposite directions." (*Researches in Molecular Dissymmetry. Lecture delivered before the Société Chimique de Paris,* 1869, p. 29.)

In the presence of this confirmation, which fulfilled his highest hopes, Pasteur was seized with such emotion that he was forced to leave his library on a run, and flung his arms around the first of his colleagues whom he met, in his keen joy over this essential discovery. He broke the news to Biot, who for long years had been studying the rotary power of crystals, by notifying him that he was ready to communicate the results of his experiments. The aged scientist and member of the Institute accepted his young colleague's offer, and the scene which took place between them was one of real beauty. It has been admirably recorded by M. Vallery-Radot:

'The meeting took place at the College de France, where Biot lived. Every slightest detail of that interview must have remained fixed forever in Pasteur's memory. Biot began by going in search of paratartaric acid.

"'I have studied it,' he said, 'with particular care: it is perfectly neutral in relation to polarised light.' A tinge of mistrust was visible in his gestures and betrayed itself in the tone of his voice. 'I will bring you everything you need,' continued the old man as he went in quest of the required quantities of soda and ammonia. He desired that the double salt should be prepared in his presence.

"After pouring the liquid obtained into the crystalliser, Biot took it and set it aside in one corner of his apartment, in order to be quite sure that no one would touch it. 'I will notify you when you are to come back,' he said to Pasteur as he ushered him out. Forty-eight hours later the crystals, very small at first, began to take form. When there appeared to be a sufficient quantity of them Pasteur was summoned. Still in the presence of Biot, Pasteur drew out the finest crystals, one by one, wiped them in order to remove the mother liquid adhering to them, then pointed out to Biot the opposition of their hemihedric character and separated them into two groups: right crystals and left crystals.

"'You claim,' said Biot, 'that the crystals placed on your right will deflect the plane of polarisation to the right and that the crystals placed on your left will deflect it to the left?'

"'Yes,' replied Pasteur.

"'Very well, I will attend to the rest.'

"Biot prepared the solutions, and once again sent for Pasteur. Biot began by placing in the apparatus the solution which was supposed to deflect to the left. When the deflection was verified he took Pasteur by the arm and uttered the phrase which has so often been cited and which deserves to become famous: 'My dear boy, I have loved science so dearly all my life that this sets my heart beating!'

"'As a matter of fact,' Pasteur afterwards said, in recalling this interview, 'it was evident that the most vivid light had been thrown upon the cause of the phenomenon of rotary polarisation and on the hemihedrism of crystals; that a new class of isomeric substances had been discovered; that the unexpected and hitherto unexampled formation of racemic or paratartaric acid had been unveiled; in a word, that a great path, new and unforeseen, had been opened to science.'" (*La Vie de Pasteur.*)

The encouragements of his masters, Balard and Biot, their praises, and the certainty that he would not be obliged to interrupt the sequence of his discoveries kept him in a state of feverish activity. But at the end of 1848 he was obliged to leave the laboratory, in spite of the intervention of his protectors, and betake himself to the Lycée at Dijon, to which he had been appointed professor of physics. It was not without regret that he abandoned his experimental courses and his researches, for he felt that his personal labours were of more use to science than any instruction that he might give. Nevertheless, he submitted to the order of the Minister of Instruction and, from the moment that he was installed, applied himself to a conscientious fulfilment of the duties of his new function. He proved himself to be a methodical and painstaking professor, seeking above all things to be clear in expounding the science that he taught, and, far from priding himself on the superiority of his own intelligence, he spent long hours in preparing his lectures, in order to make them easily comprehensible to his young students. Nevertheless, in spite of his faithful performance of his duties as a public instructor, he was not without regret for the days that he must spend outside of the laboratory. This inactivity in regard to his personal researches weighed so heavily upon him that he asked to be transferred, some months after his arrival at Dijon, and, upon being appointed to the Faculty of Strasburg as substitute professor of chemistry, was able to take possession of his new office on the 15th of

January, 1849, and to continue his researches. in spite of the scanty equipment that he had at his disposal.

An event of great importance in the life of Pasteur awaited him at Strasburg, and one which was destined to have a most fortunate influence upon his whole career as a scientist. For it was here that he was soon to find domestic happiness. From his very first visit to the president of the Faculty, M. Laurent, he conceived a strong partiality for one of the daughters, Mlle Marie Laurent. With that prevision which was characteristic of him, he was straightway convinced that this young lady was the one essential to his hearth and home, and, having once made up his mind, he acted with his customary prompt decision and asked her hand in marriage. Between his arrival in Strasburg and this request less than fifteen days had intervened! M. Laurent, to whom he presented a short note setting forth, with admirable sincerity, his financial status, his position in the University and his ambitions, accepted him as son-in-law. This was a day to be marked with a white stone, for Mme Pasteur, down to the last day of her husband's life, never ceased to surround him with the tenderest and most devoted care, to watch over his hours of toil and his hours of rest, and to keep him in such a state that he could employ his genius to the full extent of its powers.

Louis Pasteur remained on the Faculty of Strasburg until 1854, and was appointed titular professor of chemistry in 1852. This whole period is marked by numerous researches, which form the natural sequence of those that he undertook in crystalography, but which extend far beyond that science, thanks to the new perceptions that he brought to them and the consequences which naturally developed from them.

From this same aspect of dissymmetry and hemihedrism, he studied the aspartates and the malates, shed light upon obscure questions which no chemist before had successfully handled, established the laws of molecular dissymmetry, and took up and solved the problem of dissymmetry in cellular life.

Pasteur continued to address memoranda to the Academy of Sciences, and the learned world began to be stirred by these communications, which proved him to be an investigator endowed with genius. The most celebrated members of the Institute followed his progress with sympathetic interest, men such as Dumas, whom as a young student he could not hear lecture at the Sorbonne without emotion, Biot, Balard, Regnault, and Senarmont; and it occurred to them to elect him as corresponding member of the Academy of Sciences. During a visit of the illustrious scientist, Metscherlich, to Paris, Louis Pasteur had the pleasure of showing the results he had obtained to the German crystalographer, who thanked and congratulated him, and informed him that the extremely rare racemic acid was still manufactured in Germany. At this news Pasteur's zeal caught fire, and, since it was vacation time, he set forth, in September, 1852, on the pursuit of this singular substance which had once been obtained by accident at Thann, which had since been lost sight of, and which he was now informed was to be found at a manufactory of chemical products in Saxony.

There followed a mad chase throughout the length and breadth of Germany. Louis Pasteur kept a journal of his varied adventures, which he sent to his wife and which reveals his passionate ardor, his immense desire to possess at last this acid which had once astonished the scientific world. The chase was a heroic one. Pasteur went from Leipzig to Zwichau, from Zwichau to Dresden, from Dresden to Freiberg, from Freiberg to Vienna, from Vienna to Prague, filled alternately with emotions of hope and despair, according as he thought that he had found racemic acid, or that the elusive substance still seemed to evade him. "I will pursue it for ten years, if need be," he wrote to Mme Pasteur.

His researches, his experiments in the manufactories, his inquiries did not hinder him from visiting the museums, and here it was that the artistic side of his nature found satisfaction. In Dresden he kept a record of the paintings which pleased him, and he made notes which show the degree of his admiration for each of them. Pasteur debated the question of going all the way to Venice in order to obtain crude tartar which contained the rare acid, but he returned to France without having made this extra journey and very much fatigued by his long ramblings. He had convinced himself that racemic acid existed in tartar that had not been washed and that it was to be found in the mother liquid. Hence his pursuit had not been unprofitable.

Upon returning to his laboratory in Strasburg, Pasteur undertook a task which it seemed to him would be difficult to realise, but which was not beyond his powers. He had decided that this racemic acid which no other chemist had produced should issue from his own laboratory! With this ambitious design he began experiments of unimagined delicacy, working with confidence, although the master chemists whom he had told of his intent believed that he could not succeed. He was destined to triumph; the magician was about to vanquish nature. In June, 1853, he announced to his father and to Biot that he had artificially obtained racemic acid. It was a splendid victory, which amazed all scientists versed in the study of crystals and of chemistry. The Academy of Sciences gave prolonged attention to this discovery, and the Society of Chemistry bestowed upon its author a prize of fifteen hundred francs, which it had offered to anyone who should produce this extraordinary acid. With his usual disinterestedness, Pasteur spent half of this sum in the purchase of such instruments as were lacking in the Strasburg laboratory. The government took notice of the achievements of the young scientist that were so magnificently crowned by a success which his own masters had not expected, and Louis Pasteur received the cross of the Legion of Honour when he was barely thirty years of age.

[1] Pasteur, the *History of a Mind,* by E. Ducalux, p. 40.

Chapter Three - On the Road to Fame

IT needs only a brief examination in order to realise that the works of Pasteur, even those most widely different in appearance, follow one another like the links of a chain and present an admirable unity. Towards the end of his studies of crystals his ideas became generalised, and extended his theory of molecular dissymmetry to the constitution of the universe, while a certain laboratory experiment was destined to turn his attention to ferments. Having broken a crystal of tartrate, Pasteur plunged it again into the mother liquid, and, discovering that the crystal became restored in its entirety, he compared this breakage to a wound which is healed with the help of new molecules of its own kind. On the other hand, he had observed that the tartrates undergo veritable fermentations, and he believed that these fermentations might be due to a microscopic organism which played the role of a ferment; so that, setting forth from crystalography, he finally arrived at researches into the origin of life.

Having been appointed Professor of Chemistry and Dean of the Faculty recently founded at Lille in 1854, Pasteur, while faithfully fulfilling his pedagogical duties, prepared to carry on his studies of fermentations. He spared no pains to prove himself worthy of the confidence placed in him by M. Fortoul, the Minister of Public Instruction, and he succeeded in raising the new Faculty entrusted to him to the first rank of scientific establishments. More than two hundred auditors attended his courses, and twenty-one students were enrolled for practical work in the laboratory. He exerted himself to carry out the programme of the Minister, whose desire was to train operators and practical workers in the higher manufacturing industries, but he never ceased to repeat that nothing counted apart from theory, and that theory alone could be productive of great results. At the same time Pasteur initiated his students into industrial methods by taking them to visit the manufacturers of the neighbourhood, where they were able to judge at first hand which were the best of the methods employed. Furthermore, the General Council of the North recognised the practical value of his knowledge and his teaching by entrusting him with the examination of the fertilisers essential to agriculture.

The problem of fermentations which Pasteur was preparing to solve victoriously was even more obscure than those offered by crystalography. How did the heavy dough, formed of flour mixed with water, become the light and substantial bread; how was the crushed grape transformed into wine? Undoubtedly these questions had occupied the attention of man ever since the most remote antiquity, and many answers were made to them, but no answer that was scientifically satisfactory.

The alchemists of the middle ages thought that yeast had a certain power of transmutation and that fermentation, if applied to metals, would enable them to transmute a base metal, such as iron, into a precious metal, such as gold. The first of all to approach the truth was Paracelsus, who compared fermentations to diseases, but his idea was still vague, and not based upon experiments. We must wait until we come down to Lavoisier in order to see fermentations studied upon a basis of facts, but neither this great chemist nor those who followed him, Gay-Lussac, Cagniard-Latour, Schwann, Helmholtz, Liebig, succeeded in demonstrating their real origin. The theory most generally accepted, at the time when Pasteur began his researches, was that of Liebig, who attributed fermentations to matter in the course of decomposition, which played the role of a ferment in the mediums into which they were introduced.

It was in a sugar refinery at Lille, owned by M. Bigo, that Pasteur entered upon the study of fermentations. He approached it equipped with all the knowledge acquired through his work in the tartrates, which must have singularly aided him to reach a solution of the problem that had been so long and vainly sought. We cannot follow him through these delicate and difficult experiments, but he arrived at this luminous and unforeseen conclusion that fermentation was not a phenomenon of death, as Liebig had thought it, but a phenomenon of life, and this he proved in an irrefutable manner.

His experiments, which were directed more especially to lactic and alcoholic fermentation, showed him that all fermentation was due to the presence of living cells which alone were the active agents of the transformation. These cells had a life of their own, and the phenomena of fermentations were closely connected with it and influenced by the different phases of its evolution, according as these cells were ill, dying or in full vigour. This was indeed a light thrown upon what had hitherto been nothing but darkness, a discovery which was destined to create an entire new science and of which the consequences were at that time incalculable.

The scientific associations, both in France and abroad, disturbed at first by Pasteur's farsighted genius and by the unforeseen results of his researches, awaited his communications with something bordering upon impatience. He received recognition beyond any of the other young investigators, for he had proved himself to be one of those with whom it was henceforth necessary to reckon. He began to receive recompenses. In 1857 the Royal Society of London bestowed upon him the great Rumford medal for his work in crystalography, and the same year his friends in the Institute, and Biot among the first, who felt a paternal affection for him, urged him to present himself as a candidate for the Academy of Sciences in the section of mineralogy. Pasteur accepted this flattering invitation from the masters of his profession, who now looked upon him as at least their equal, but he made a rather sorry candidate, being too fond of truth and justice to be willing to play upon those little human vanities which assure success in all elections. Accordingly, in spite of Senarmont's report, which was highly eulogistic of Pasteur's discoveries, insisting upon their value and importance, Pasteur received only sixteen votes.

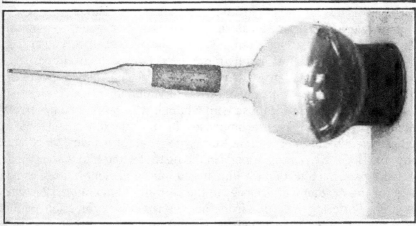

PASTEUR AT THE AGE OF THIRTY - In 1852, the great scientist was appointed titular professor of chemistry at Strasburg, where he conducted a number of researches in crystalography. To the left is one of the glass globes which were employed in certain celebrated experiments relating to spontaneous generation.

He took his way back to Lille, not greatly cast down by a defeat which he had foreseen, but he remained there only a short time, because, on the opening of the scholastic year of 1857, he was appointed Administrator of the École Normale and director of the scientific studies, while Nisard assumed the general direction.

Henceforth this was to be the centre of Pasteur's life, his whole life of toil, of combats on behalf of science and humanity, and his family life as well, a very happy one, notwithstanding that it was destined to be marked by some inevitable bereavements which his profound faith as a Catholic aided him to bear. It was from the little laboratory in the Rue d'Ulm that the great and peaceful revolution was to proceed, designed to cure all the ills of life by penetrating the secrets of nature. It ought to be regarded as a sacred spot, for one of the finest of all human minds lived and thought there, while such high virtues as courage, perseverance and moral strength were there put into magnificent practice.

M. Maurice de Fleury has related how Pasteur never ceased working, even when his laborious day was ended:

"During fifteen years," he says, "he could be seen each evening after dinner pacing up and down a long corridor where no one dared to come and interrupt his reverie. Paralysed since 1870 — for on two different occasions apoplexy attacked his brain — he would seize the bunch of keys in his pocket with his stiffened hand and make them rattle in order to soothe his thoughts with the rhythmic sound; and as he walked he slightly dragged one foot, while his mind ripened some newly conceived idea or prepared for the experiment of the morrow. At times his reverie assumed the intensity of ecstacy; and within the brain of this man of genius flashes of light revealed his goal, and gave him a prevision of ail that was destined to emanate from him.

"How beautiful it is! How beautiful it is!" he would murmur in low tones. Then, resuming his pacing with a firmer step, he would add, "I must work." And so he would continue until the hour of eleven.

Is there not something deeply touching in this picture of the great man toiling on into the night, after all the experiments he had made during the day, experiments made under very hard conditions? His laboratory in the École Normale was, as a matter of fact, exceedingly primitive and inconvenient. It consisted of two inadequate rooms which he himself had contrived in the garret, and, while it was freezing cold in winter, during the summer the temperature would rise to 97° Fahrenheit. Nevertheless, it was here that he completed his studies of fermentations, from 1857 to 1859, and notably those of alcoholic fermentation. It was here also that he was destined to discover a phenomenon which overthrew all accepted ideas regarding the essential conditions of animal life. No one had questioned that oxygen was a necessity to all animals without exception. Pasteur proceeded to prove that for certain species it was fatal, and that they died at its contact. While examining under the microscope a tiny drop of butyric fermentation, placed between two very thin sheets of glass, Pasteur observed that the bacteria known as the *vibrion,* which produce this fermentation, were very lively at the centre and furthest from the air, but that those near the border line became inert. What was he to conclude from this phenomenon, which contradicted all observations that he had previously made of various infusions, in which the animalcula left the centre of the drop in order to draw near to the margin which supplied them with more oxygen? Was it possible that there were animal forms which made an exception to a law that was supposed to be general, were there some that led an anaerobic life (*i.e.,* without oxygen), while it had previously been regarded as settled that all animals led an aerobic life, in which oxygen was a necessity? Pasteur solved this question by passing a current of air into a flask containing a butyric fermentation, and immediately the life of the *vibrions* diminished in intensity and finally ceased. The proof had been obtained that there were animal forms to which oxygen was fatal.

But how did it happen that these anaerobic *vibrions* had not met with oxygen in the medium in which they were bred? It was because the aerobic *vibrions* which preceded their evolution had exhausted all the oxygen in the liquid, and thus gave them a chance to live and multiply. Furthermore, these two forms of life were found coexisting in the same liquid, a part of the aerobic forms having died and fallen to the bottom of the vessel after exhausting the oxygen, while the more vigorous rose to the surface and continued to live, thanks to the oxygen in the air, and formed at the same time a protective layer for the anaerobics, which were thus enabled to develop in the lower depths. Pasteur was destined, later on, to study in detail these phenomena which no one before him had observed, and to gather new light from them. M. Duclaux emphasises the element of genius in these researches:

"I have tried to present all these deductions as a whole," he writes, "because as a matter of fact they were the result of a few weeks of work and meditation, and also because they afford us an example of Pasteur's power of penetration in perceiving and outlining a problem, and the patience he exhibited in gathering together the elements essential to a solution. Throughout the best years of his life this man lived in advance of his time, a pioneer lost in solitude, absorbed in the contemplation of the horizons he had discovered and which his eye alone could behold and traverse. What is less surprising than his indifference to the details of actual life? He lived in his own thoughts, without being a dreamer, for a dream which reaches its goal and produces results ceases to be a dream."

But these delicate experiments and lofty speculations did not make Pasteur forget that he was Administrator of the École Normale as well as director of scientific studies. And never did a man take his duties more seriously than he, even when they were a burden and a constraint. He applied himself to everything that he undertook with the same degree of attention and conscientiousness, and nothing seemed to him too trivial to be worthy of supervision and painstaking. Accordingly he took every pains to give a perfect administration to the great school that he still loved as well as he had done in boyhood, when it had appeared to him as the far-off goal of his highest hopes. He concerned himself about the health of the students and the hygiene of the locality, and even the smallest details were objects of his solicitude, such as airing a classroom or sanding a court. Even the scientific side of his mind found employment in his administrative role: for instance, when he undertook comparative calculations as to the number of ounces of meat furnished for each meal to the students at the Normale and the Poly technique!

This anxiety to be a good administrator in no wise interfered with his researches. He accepted the additional burden without complaint, and his scientific activity was in no wise retarded. In the same manner that crystals led him to fermentations it was these latter which were destined to lead him to studies which seemed to overstep the boundary of science and to enter the metaphysical domain of the origins of life, the solution of which had hitherto been the concern of philosophers rather than of scientists. When Pasteur saw, under the lens of a microscope, cells of yeast conducting themselves like living organisms, when he saw the *vibrions* moving, growing and dying, he straightway asked himself where these yeasts and these *vibrions* come from. Are they born spontaneously from matter in a state of decomposition, or is it not more likely that, in accordance with the general laws of life, they are produced by germs? This was, in short, the question of spontaneous generation, which had so long been combatted and which he now undertook to solve. Pasteur believed that nothing is self-creative, but this was something which had to be proved, and he succeeded in proving it victoriously, in the full heat of battle, and in spite of the attacks and insults of those who championed the opposite doctrine.

His friends, with Biot at their head, tried to turn him aside from these researches, which they judged useless and vain. But Pasteur, strong in his conviction and with that dogged will which never turned back from any obstacle, so long as he was sure that he had grasped the truth, disregarded the advice of his elders and plunged into experiments that bristled with difficulties.

From the most remote antiquity spontaneous generation had been accepted, and it is well known that the ancients believed that eels were born from the slime of river banks, and that it did not seem to them impossible that bees should issue from the decomposing entrails of a bull. Without going quite so far back, we find that the great naturalist, Buff on, supported the theory of spontaneous generation; but the first experiments to prove its truth were made by an Irishman, Needham, in the eighteenth century. Enclosing putrefying matter in a vessel which he sealed hermetically, and heating the whole apparatus in hot ashes, in order to destroy all living germs, he allowed the vessel to become cold, and after the lapse of several days he found that it contained animalcula. This went to prove that spontaneous generation had taken place. Spallanzani repeated these experiments, and, after heating the closed vessel to a higher degree, observed that no animalcula afterwards developed. Needham rejoined that by using too high a degree of heat he had killed the *vegetative force* from which creation proceeded. None of these experiments was conclusive, and, although they were repeated by Gay-Lussac, Schulze and Schwann, their results remained uncertain and often contradictory.

When Pasteur intervened the theory of spontaneous generation was supported by Pouchet, and it may be said that it was accepted by a considerable number of scientists. It is true, however, that no decisive evidence had been offered either for or against the theory. It was at this moment that Pasteur revealed himself, not only as a man of daring and profound thought, but as the most careful and experienced of operators. To those who believed in spontaneous generation he said, "Everything comes from a germ, and even these animalcula, which seem to you to have been born spontaneously in the infusions in which they develop, come quite simply from germs and spores which are floating in the air. You have conducted your experiments badly; I will begin them over again, and I will prove to you that the substances which you regard as subject to decay are not so when they are rigorously sheltered from the air."

Pasteur began his experiments at the end of 1859, and he pursued them in the midst of the din of battle, for his adversaries disputed his conclusions in advance. The contest lasted for more than four years, with attacks, counter-attacks and violent battles, but finally the victory remained with Pasteur, without even his most bitter enemies venturing to dispute him further.

Assailing his problem at its foundation, he proved the actual existence of germs and spores in the atmosphere; then he conceived of a distribution of glass globes which would enable him to demonstrate by experiment what he had already maintained against the supporters of spontaneous generation. Pasteur declared that germs are unevenly distributed in the atmosphere, and that the air of high mountain tops contains either few or none at all; Pouchet and Joly, on the contrary, contended that air, by its own nature, could cause spontaneous generation in any and every locality. Both parties made experiments in their own behalf, and each experiment gave different results. These polemics spread beyond scientific circles to the daily press, and, since the question of religion was involved, the public took sides for the one party or the other, according to their individual opinions, the results obtained by Pasteur being regarded as conforming with the biblical account of the creation, while those of Pouchet seemed to invalidate and contradict it.

For his first demonstration Pasteur employed globes with a curving neck, into which he introduced an infusion liable to putrefy, either of hay or of malt, which had been brought to the boiling point in order to destroy whatever germs it might contain; and, having done this, he left the globes exposed to the open air. No disturbances took place in the infusion, but if, by tipping the globes, he brought the liquid into contact with the walls of the curved neck, after a longer or shorter time the infusion would begin to swarm with life, thus furnishing a double proof, first, that pure air has no effect upon liquids subject to putrefaction, and, secondly, that it was the germs and spores heavier than the air which had been deposited in the curved neck that gave birth to the infusoria popularly attributed to spontaneous generation.

On the other side, Pouchet declared that the air, being everywhere the same, had the power, no matter where it was gathered, of causing the creation of *vibrions,* through its action upon liquids subject to putrefaction; while Pasteur continued to maintain that germs and spores were unequally distributed in the atmosphere, and that, if the air was taken from the mountain tops, it was impossible that it should disturb the liquids brought into contact with it, since there would be a complete absence of germs and spores. The experiments which Pasteur made, as simple as they are conclusive, to demonstrate the truth of his conception, have remained historic. It was through the aid of globes with a straight neck finely drawn out that he ultimately succeeded; and this is the way that he achieved his proof, thanks to his practical qualities as an experimenter of extreme caution who never left anything to chance.

After having half-filled his globes with some alterable liquid, such as an infusion of brewer's yeast, Pasteur brought it to the boiling point, and, when the steam had driven out ail the air, he quickly closed the point of the finely drawn-out neck by means of a blow-pipe. The globes thus prepared — the liquid being contained in an almost absolute vacuum — were transported to various different localities, and then opened with infinite precautions: the fine point of the neck was broken with pincers previously heated in a flame, the air re-entered the globes, which were immediately sealed again and placed in ovens, where they were subjected to a temperature of 86 degrees Fahrenheit. The liquid behaved differently, according to the locality from which the air had been obtained, the fermentation being very rapid if it had come from a neighbourhood where there was much dust, much slower when it was taken, for instance, from the cellar of the Observatory, and in some cases there was no alteration at all.

In spite of these results, Pasteur's experiments continued to be disputed. He resolved to undertake a scientific campaign, against which his adversaries should no longer be able to stand out. Armed with sixty-three globes, he set forth, in September, 1860, for the mountain heights of the Alps. He halted first at Arbois, where he took some specimens of air; then from Mount Poujet he proceeded to Chamounix, and there he opened some of his globes on the Mer de Glace. There, in that pure air, far from human crowds, germs and spores ought either not to exist or else to be very rare. The results proved that he was right. Out of twenty globes opened on the mountain heights nineteen remained sterile, while in the case of those into which air was admitted at lower levels the proportion of sterile ones, out of the same number, fell off to fifteen and to twelve. The proof was decisive.

But Pouchet, his bitterest opponent, having repeated the same experiments, only with a less degree of care, arrived at different results, and denied the value of Pasteur's demonstrations. He also had obtained air from various localities, even from Sicily, and there, just as elsewhere, he had found it fertile, and ready to act upon liquids capable of putrefying. The conflict assumed epic proportions. The sessions of the Academy of Sciences caught the echoes of it, each theory having its partizans, and each experimenter his enemies. Pasteur, however, ended by convincing the learned assemblage, which in 1862 awarded him a prize for his *Memorandum on Organic Corpuscles existing in the Atmosphere.* Alone, or almost alone, Pouchet, Joly and Musset refused to lay down arms, and continued to carry on an active war. In order to force them to surrender Pasteur requested the Academy of Sciences to name a commission to judge between him and his adversaries, each party being required to repeat their experiments in the presence of the commissioners chosen. Pouchet, Joly and Musset accepted, but on the day appointed for the tests they announced that they had failed, while Pasteur, accompanied by Duclaux, arrived bringing his globes and his liquids with him. The experiment was a success, and Baland recorded, in the name of the Commission, the conclusive results, in the *Comtes Rendus de l'Academie des Sciences.* After a hard campaign of several years Pasteur was at last triumphant.

This question of spontaneous generation aroused an interest outside of the men of science. It had called attention to the mysterious world of infinitely little things, and people were eager to gather around the microscope in order to see these redoubtable organisms, the full extent of whose power was as yet unknown. Pasteur had obtained the concession of a suite of five rooms in the École Normale, to be used as a laboratory. Having thus been enabled to quit his garret, he began to receive illustrious visitors, statesmen, society women, personages of high standing at court, all of whom came to beg him to initiate them into the secrets which he had discovered, and of which he seemed to be the sole guardian.

During his researches in spontaneous generation Pasteur had received from the Academy of Sciences, in 1860, the prize for experimental physiology, and in 1861 he had for a second time presented himself as a candidate in the section of botany. He was supported by his faithful friend Biot, but, nevertheless, he obtained only 24 votes. He was not destined to be elected until the 8th of December, 1862, with a majority of 36 out of a total of sixty votes, to the section of mineralogy, where he succeeded Senarmont.

Pasteur was now celebrated, acclaimed by some, and combatted by others who were unable to comprehend the utterly new order of his genius. Napoleon III expressed his desire to meet him, and it was his first master, Dumas, the one who had formerly caused Pasteur such keen emotion by his lectures on chemistry at the Sorbonne, who presented him to the Emperor at the Tuileries in March, 1863.

Pasteur delighted Napoleon III by his serious and simple manner. He explained his ideas regarding the scientific problems on which he was engaged, and confessed to the Emperor that his most secret ambition was to study contagious diseases in order to find a cure for all humanity.

Chapter Four - For the National Wealth

THE campaign which Pasteur was conducting against spontaneous generation did not absorb his entire activity. He pursued his studies of fermentation, striving to penetrate the secrets of the infinitely small, the yeasts, the vibrions, the infusoria, that whole disquieting world, the universal and formidable activity of which was not even yet suspected. Perhaps he already discerned, although only vaguely, their presence in human diseases, and this was the object of his researches and profound meditations.

Pasteur used to arrive at his laboratory, walking slowly, sunk in thought, and with his forehead lined with care. He gave orders to his assistants, pointing out the experiments which he wished to have made, but never revealing the idea behind them. Succeeding Raulin, he had Duclaux, who was still young and who was destined to become a great scientist. Duclaux admired the achievements of his master, and with his keen and lucid mind followed his luminous trail, while he often added to his duties as assistant the humbler ones of a laboratory attendant, wiping the apparatus, the retorts and flasks, a devoted servant in the temple of science. A rather sorry temple, by the way, for the laboratory was extremely inconvenient, with its five scanty rooms and a stove installed behind the staircase, where Pasteur could not enter except on his knees. Duclaux compared it to a rabbit cage, "and yet it was from there," he said, "that the movement started which revolutionized science."

Already at that epoch a large faction of the younger generation of scientists had come under the daily increasing influence of Pasteur. "The Normal School chemists of 1860," wrote Mrs. Duclaux, in her *Vie d'Émile Duclaux*, "believed in Pasteur as the romantics of 1830 believed in Victor Hugo. They saw before them virgin lands and unimagined sources. Thanks to the genius, the faith and the religious spirit that the master infused into his work, he inspired these younger men with his own enthusiasm, and they believed themselves born to revolutionise the ideas which had served as dogmas for their predecessors; and such a belief is strangely intoxicating to young brains! Among the assistants and students who gathered around M. Pasteur in the little laboratory in the Rue d'Ulm, there was a continual interchange of conceptions and of projects — very different ones from those that are born and die daily apropos of literature or philosophy, for these discussions dealt with the only form of truth that is capable of being verified, namely science."

But, while Pasteur kept secret the object he had in view during the course of his experiments that were often long, difficult and countless times recommenced, when he had once obtained his results he boldly and vigorously proclaimed them. He had a scorn of bad faith, routine and prejudice, and everyone knows the famous apostrophe which he addressed to his adversaries who were disputing his discoveries in relation to the crystals of tartrates at a meeting of the Société Philomatique on the eighth of December, 1862: "If you have ever known anything of the subject, what have you done with your knowledge? And, if you have not known, why do you interfere?" He was a rough antagonist, but he fought only for the triumph of truth, putting all personal considerations aside.

In the course of his studies of fermentations Pasteur was led to study the phenomenon through which wine was transformed into vinegar. The celebrated chemist, Liebig, had established a theory which did not altogether agree with his own observations, and he proceeded victoriously to advance his own theory in opposition.

The manufacturers of vinegar in Orléans pursued the following method: Into groups of stationary barrels they poured a mixture of two-thirds ripened vinegar and one-third wine. On the surface of this mixture there was formed a thin film, of which no one knew the composition, but which was necessary in order to obtain a prompt and thorough acetification, or transformation into vinegar. The manufacturers took great care of this film, for, if it was dislodged or if it sank to the bottom of the barrels, the whole operation had to be done over. What was this film which, in order to work well, required a current of fresh air that was furnished by drilling an opening in the barrels a little above the level of the liquid? Pasteur worked for nearly a year on this problem, and he proved that acetification was caused by a microbe which, living on the surface of the liquid, obtained oxygen from the air and transferred a part of it to the liquid below, which in this way was oxidised. He gave this microbe the name of *mycoderma aceti,* or mycoderm of vinegar. This ferment is endowed with an extraordinary power of prolificness. The individual cells, twice as long as they are wide, are so minute that it requires 400 of them, placed end to end, and 800, placed side by side, to measure a millimetre in length, that thirty million can find space in a square centimetre, and three hundred billion are formed in twenty-four hours upon a square metre of the liquid! What is the weight of these three hundred billions of cells? One gram, and this gram is capable of transforming ten kilograms of alcohol into vinegar in the space of five days. It follows that a single cell consumes, in the course of one day, a quantity of nourishment equal to two thousand times its own weight. From these fabulous figures one can form some conception of the activity of these infinitely small organisms and of their formidable power in the economy of universal life.

Pasteur discovered that the mycoderm of wine could become ill and that it produced either good or bad vinegar as the case might be. Through proper cultivation he obtained perfect cells which, when placed in a mixture of wine and vinegar, produced an excellent and regular acetification. Up to this time the industry of the vinegar makers of Orléans was subject to all sorts of losses due to ignorance and to chance. Pasteur furnished them with a method which never failed. He saved them from the daily anxiety of obtaining bad products, and he helped them to gain millions.

At the same time that he was occupied with vinegars Pasteur had been investigating even as far back as 1863 the origin of different maladies which affect wines. The municipal counsel of Arbois, priding themselves on this illustrious compatriot, offered him a laboratory where he might pursue these studies that were of interest to all the wine growers of France. Pasteur preferred to be installed in independent quarters; and Duclaux, who on several occasions directed the experiments made at Arbois, has given a most picturesque description of the place. The laboratory had been established in a former café:

'The traditional signboard had been left above the entrance, in consequence of which it often happened to us to have customers enter and ask for food and drinks. Generally they halted at the door, surprised at the strangeness of the furnishings, and took themselves off without a word, assuredly carrying with them visions of the almanac of Nostradamus. It must be said in their defense that, if the room no longer resembled a cafe, it resembled a laboratory quite as little. There was no gas; the heating was done with coal, the flames of which were made more active at the required moment with the help of fans. There was no water; we ourselves went, like Rebecca, to draw it at the public fountain, or, like Nausicaä, to wash our utensils by the river bank. Our tables were trestles, and as for our apparatus, since nearly all of it came from the local carpenter, tinsmith or blacksmith of Arbois, it may be imagined that they did not have the canonical forms and that, when we walked through the streets on our way to the wine cellars to get the wine for the purpose of analysis, we did not pass by without calling forth some sarcastic comments from the somewhat hostile inhabitants of the little town.

Whatever this haphazard workshop may have been, Pasteur's experiments, methodically and perseveringly continued, were decisive. What was the cause of the maladies of wines? Contrary to the widely accepted opinions, Pasteur proved that oxygen was not injurious to wine, but that, on the contrary, it was oxygen which aged it and gave it flavour and bouquet. Wine hermetically sealed, without contact with oxygen, remained forever young. This prejudice having been overcome by experiments, Pasteur showed further that each malady of wine had its own special microbe and that under the microscope it was possible to distinguish those of *la tourne,* of *l'amer,* of *la graisse,* all of them well-known maladies of wine, but by no means the only ones.

How was it possible to combat these microbes, the terrors of wine growers and epicures, for no barrel and no bottle was surely safe? Pasteur tried at first to use antiseptics, tasteless and odourless, but without obtaining good results. It was through the application of heat that he finally solved the problem, and it was well worth the solving, since the vineyards of France produce as a matter of fact fifty million hectolitres of an average value of five hundred million francs, and suffer enormous losses through the occurrence of diseases.

Pasteur heated the wines in a closed vessel to 130 degrees Fahrenheit, and by thus destroying the microbes put them in a condition to be kept without danger of spoiling. But this process of heating had to contend with many prejudices. It was believed that it altered the quality of the wines, and the wine growers were reluctant to adopt this method of preservation. A commission was appointed to try the effect of the Pasteur method upon wines to be transported by sea. They put on board the *Jean-Bart* at Brest samples of wine that had been heated and other samples that had not been heated. After ten months of ocean travel the former samples were declared by the commission to be excellent in all respects, while the latter samples had turned sour. The experiment was repeated on board the frigate *La Sibylle,* and gave the same results. The wine that had been heated preserved all its characteristic qualities and escaped all injury. For that matter the protection of liquids by heating has now become general and we *pasteurise* milk, beer, etc.

Napoleon III became interested in Pasteur's study of wines, for it involved the question of safeguarding one of the principal sources of the wealth of France. Accordingly, during one of the sojourns of the court at Compiègne both he and the Empress, Eugénie, were initiated into the details of the experiments. It was in 1865 that Pasteur, armed with his microscope and his samples of wine, delivered a lecture on the subject before the emperor and empress, and taught them to distinguish, with their eye at the lense, the microbes of the *tourne* from those of the *amer.* Napoleon III expressed surprise that it had not occurred to Pasteur to make a pecuniary profit out of his discoveries, which were worth tens of millions to the wine industry, and Pasteur made this fine response: "In France a scientist would think that he had demeaned himself if he did such a thing." According to his standards, they must content themselves with glory and with the satisfaction of a duty fulfilled.

In Pasteur, Napoleon III liked both the man and the scientist, and many a time he invited him either to the Tuileries or to Compiegne. Arrangements were made to conduct some experiments in the apartments of the empress, and in the presence of the ladies of honour Pasteur expounded the mysteries of the world of infinitely little things. Incidentally he met with a singular adventure, which might have banished him from the Court, if the affection which the Empress bore him had been less genuine. For the purposes of a certain demonstration Pasteur had needed some live frogs, which he had obtained from the head gardener of the parks at Compiegne. When the experiment was ended the absent-minded scientist left the frogs behind him, imprisoned in an insecure bag. They invaded the bed chamber of the Empress, and the latter, arising during the night, set her foot upon a cold and slimy

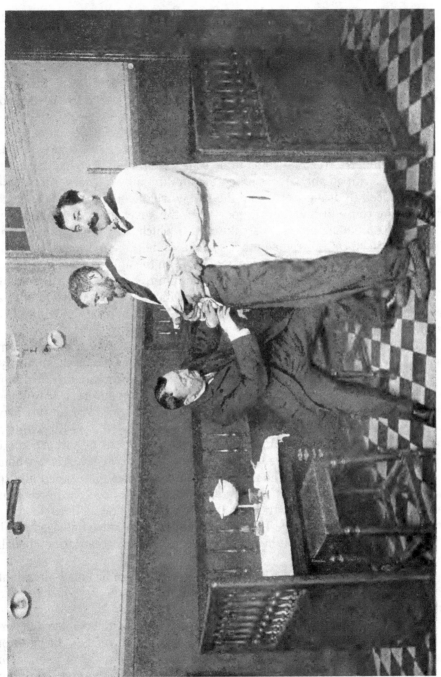

VACCINATION AGAINST HYDROPHOBIA - One of the rooms in the Institute, in which, thanks to Pasteur's genius, the virus of one of the most terrible scourges in the world is rendered impotent. Through this discovery, Pasteur is enrolled in the number of the great benefactors of humanity.

frog. She experienced a terrible fright and very nearly fainted. Afterwards she laughed at her own fear, but, although she bore no grudge against Pasteur, she could never again bear even the sight of the poor, inoffensive frog!

In 1867 Pasteur received from the jury of the Exposition Universelle a grand prize for his services in behalf of wines. But even before these researches were fully completed he had prepared to undertake a new series of studies that were destined to enhance his fame still further.

For fifteen years a veritable scourge had ravaged the departments of southern France. The industry of rearing silk-worms, formerly so prosperous that the mulberry tree had come to be called *the tree of gold,* had fallen off alarmingly, with an annual loss of more than fifty million francs. The people were reduced to dire poverty, and the sorely tried land owners, helpless to combat the cause of their ruin, appealed to the government. Strange maladies were spreading among the silk-worms, which died in countless numbers, and there was no remedy that seemed to help them. Dumas, commissioned to present to the Senate the petition from the affected district, having confidence in the genius of Pasteur, begged him to consent to go and study on the spot this disease of the silk-worms, which was proving so fatal to a national industry that in the single district of Alais it had caused within five years a loss of nearly a hundred and fifty million francs.

Pasteur knew nothing of the subject, but in the face of such a permanent menace, which condemned a whole section of France to the blackest misery, he consented to absent himself from his beloved laboratory in the Rue d'Ulm and to accept the commission from the Ministry of Agriculture. It was in the midst of sorrow and mourning that he was destined to carry on this new study — a long and difficult one, lasting from 1865 to 1870 — for within a few years he lost his father and two of his daughters. His father! We know the profound affection that he felt for the old soldier of the Empire, to whom he owed his love for work and that steadfast conscience that guided him so straightly through the path of life. His daughters! The joy and the hope of his home circle. These intimate tragedies traced a few additional lines upon his austere face, but it was with the same valiant heart, the same unbiased mind, the same tenacious will that he continued to pursue his great task on behalf of humanity.

Pasteur left Paris in the early days of June, 1865, and installed himself at Pont-Biquet, in a small silk-worm farm near Alais, in the very heart of the stricken district.

The diseases of silk-worms had already been studied by Guérin-Menneville, Lebert and Frey, Osimo, Cantoni and de Quatrefages, the latter of whom gave its name to the most redoubtable of these diseases, *pébrine*. In this disease the bodies of the infected worms became covered over with spots resembling grains of pepper. It was known in a vague way that it was caused by corpuscles, but, when it became a question of determining their nature and the manner of their invasion, there was nothing but darkness and contradictions. As for remedies, they were purely empirical; resort was had to sulphur, sugar, ground mustard, ashes, etc., and all of them were quite in vain.

Pasteur had to find his way through an inextricable labyrinth, without any special knowledge, and armed solely with his intuitive mind and his unrivalled qualities as an investigator. In his *Histoire d'un Esprit* Duclaux, who, together with Gernez and Maillot, was his collaborator at Pont-Biquet, relates all the fluctuations of that six years' struggle, with its mistakes, its hopes, and its discouragements, surrounded by the indifference and the hostility of those whose interests it disturbed, and the final triumph, assured, indisputable and universally acclaimed.

At the very beginning Pasteur made the mistake of thinking that the corpuscles were the result of *pébrine* and that they did not make their appearance until the disease had reached a certain stage. But, notwithstanding that he was wrong in this, he established the fact that corpusculous moths produced corpusculous eggs, and that the whole problem was to find a way of obtaining healthy eggs. In this way he opened up the path to the truth. After experiments of unimagined delicacy which demanded ceaseless watchfulness, Pasteur convinced himself that the corpuscles were not an effect of the disease, but its cause, a form of parasite that invaded the bodies of the silkworms. He proved that *pébrine* was hereditary and contagious, and that the variations that were shown to occur in the disease were due solely to the state of receptivity of the individual insects, according as they were more or less sensitive to the action of the parasite. Here we have in embryo the theory of microbic diseases, which was destined a few years later to revolutionise the science of medicine.

Pasteur converted himself into a cultivator of silk-worms, and, after many alternations between success and defeat, he obtained eggs that were perfectly healthy. His method was simple. After the moths had finished laying he reduced their bodies to a pulp, and examined them under a microscope, and every batch of eggs that was thus shown to have come from a corpusculous moth was destroyed. This operation, although so simple, encountered desperate opposition on the. part of vendors of silkworm eggs, with whose trade it interfered. It required all of Pasteur's energy to overcome this opposition, and all his activity as well, for he had to respond to all the appeals of the silk producers who sought his eggs or his advice as to the best methods to follow. A campaign of insults and calumnies was organised against the great man, and it is even stated that he once had to seek safety in Alais, followed by an angry mob that stoned him as he went. Pasteur was keenly sensitive to such malevolent attacks, but none the less he continued his task. Rising early in the morning, he would stand for long hours before the cases of silk-worms, making observations and recording the daily results of his experiments, never discouraged, or at least overcoming by force of will those moments when the desired goal seemed as remote as ever, and proceeding to begin his work over again, to correct his opinions in accordance with the newly observed facts, with no intention of halting until he should hold within his powerful grasp the indisputable truth!

What a heroic battle! And it must not be forgotten that Pasteur hardly knew what silkworms were when he undertook to cure them. The celebrated entomologist, Henri Fabre, relates in his *Souvenirs* the details of a visit that Pasteur paid him upon arriving in the South.

Pasteur requested to see some cocoons. Fabre brought him a handful. The illustrious scientist took them in his hand, turned and returned them, shook them near his ear, and exclaimed:

"Why, there is something inside!"

'The chrysalis," replied Fabre.

"The chrysalis! What's that?"

"A sort of mummy into which the caterpillar changes before becoming a moth."

"And inside of every cocoon there is one of those things?"

"Certainly, it is to protect the chrysalis that the caterpillar spins its co-coon."

"Ah!" responded Pasteur simply.

Is not this an admirable scene, as described by the old entomologist Fabre? Pasteur knew nothing, Pasteur worked, observed, drew deductions, came to a conclusion — and, where every one else had failed, he alone succeeded! Such is the power of genius.

The work upon silk-worms had its interruptions, for Pasteur tried to reconcile his personal researches with his functions as director of scientific studies at the École Normale. But in any case he was forced to abandon them in 1867, as the result of a small rebellion among the students, due to a discourse delivered by Sainte-Beuve before the Senate on the subject of freedom of opinion. The school had been dismissed, and the directors, Nisard, Pasteur and Jacquinet, replaced in the course of reorganisation.

The Minister of Public Instruction, Duruy, appointed Pasteur professor of chemistry at the Sorbonne, but where was he to find a new laboratory? The only adequate one at the École Normale was occupied by Sainte-Claire Deville, and it was impossible even to think of returning to the wretched quarters where the experiments on spontaneous generation had been made. Then it was that Pasteur, who, in spite of his personal modesty, was conscious of all that he was still able to do for science, requested that a laboratory should be constructed for him. This request was made in a note of such an exalted tone that it deserves to be reproduced in its entirety. It was addressed to Napoleon III.

"Sire," wrote Pasteur, "my researches in regard to fermentations and the role played by microscopic organisms have opened up to physiological chemistry new avenues of which the agricultural industries and the study of medicine have already begun to reap the fruit. But the field which remains to be

36

traversed is immense. My greatest desire would be to explore this field with renewed ardour, without being hampered by the insufficiency of material means.

"Since it involves seeking, by a patient and scientific study of putrefaction, for certain principles capable of guiding us to a discovery of the causes of putrid or contagious diseases, I should like to be installed in some building where the laboratory and its various dependencies would afford enough space to carry on the experiments comfortably and without danger to health.

"But how can researches be conducted in relation to gangrene, the viruses, and experiments in inoculation, unless we have quarters suitable for receiving animals, whether alive or dead? Butcher's meat brings an exorbitant price in Europe, but it is a superfluity in Buenos Ayres. How is it possible, in a cramped laboratory lacking in the necessary resources, to apply all the various tests to processes which, perhaps, render the preservation and transportation of meat a simple matter? The disease popularly known as *sang de rate* (splenic apoplexy) causes in the district of Beauce an annual loss of four million francs; it would be indispensable to go there, no doubt for several successive seasons, at the period of the greatest heat, and spend several weeks in the environs of Charente, in order to carry on a series of minute observations.

"These researches and a thousand others, which, according to my belief, are related to the great phenomenon of the transformation of organic matter after death and the enforced return of every living thing to the soil and the atmosphere, are compatible only with the installation of a vast laboratory. The time has come to emancipate the experimental sciences from the obstacles which trammel them." [1]

Napoleon III responded to this eloquent appeal in which Pasteur outlined, to a certain extent, the programme of his future work. He gave an order to Duruy to gratify this legitimate desire of the scientist and the Minister of Public Instruction that a laboratory should be built for him by the State in the gardens of the École Normale. But they needs must reckon with administrative delays! The plans were handed in by the architect of the École, M. Bouchot, in accordance with Pasteur's specifications, in September, 1867, but the actual work was delayed until a year later, after Pasteur had denounced, in a pamphlet, the *Budget de la Science,* the lamentable conditions under which French scientists were obliged to conduct their experiments, as compared with scientists in other countries, and notably in Germany.

Meanwhile a catastrophe was about to befall Pasteur and even menace his life. On the 19th of October, 1868, he was prostrated by an attack of paralysis on the left side, and so gravely affected that for the first twenty-four hours a fatal termination was feared. Pasteur rallied from the crisis, thanks to the robustness of his constitution; and it was during those days of physical and mental suffering, while he lay motionless, as though stricken by a thunderbolt, that he revealed most vividly the loftiness of his thoughts, the beauty of his character and the stoic grandeur of his principles. On the second afternoon of his illness Dr. Godelier, who was attending him, was enabled to make the following announcement in his health bulletin: "He wishes to talk about science." In reply to Sainte-Claire Deville, who had spoken some affectionate words of encouragement, he uttered the following admirable phrase: "I regret to die: I should like to have been of more service to my country." His preoccupation as a scientist never for an instant left him, as Dr. Godelier himself attested, and eight days after his attack he dictated a note to M. Gernez, his assistant, in relation to the diseases of silkworms.

Pasteur was surrounded with the most devoted care by his family, and also by his pupils, who loved him as they might have loved a father who was somewhat cold, somewhat distant, but who hid beneath an external reserve a warm heart ever ready to defend his friends. Messrs. Gernex, Duclaux, Raulin, Didon and Bertin took turns in watching beside him, anxiously following the successive phases of his illness. The whole scientific world was troubled, as though facing the possibility of a great disaster, and Napoleon III himself demanded news every morning.

Six weeks after his attack Pasteur was able to rise, and entered upon his convalescence. He had been affected badly by the stoppage of the work upon his laboratory which had coincided with the beginning of his illness, but by the order of the Emperor it had been resumed, and from his window Pasteur could see the foundations beginning to rise. The hope of soon being able to recommence his experiments with the help of material means such as he had long desired hastened his cure. While he rested his body he went into a sort of spiritual retirement. He read, or had read to him, the *Thoughts* of Pascal, *The Knowledge of God and of Oneself,* and the *Works* of Nicole. This man of science, unique in his qualities as an experimenter, who would abandon any and every theory in the face of facts, always separated science from Faith, and it is known that he was a practical Catholic to the day of his death.

As soon as he could be removed Pasteur wished to return to the south of France, in order to continue his study of silk-worms, and clear up certain points which seemed to him to be still obscure. He disregarded all suggestions of prudence, and, in spite of his weakened condition, he installed himself, in January, 1869, at Saint-Hippolyte-du-Pont, near Alais. Shortly after his arrival Pasteur, who still moved his left arm and leg clumsily, fell to the ground, and once more had to take to his bed. But he none the less continued to work, dictating the experiments to be made to his collaborators, Gernez, Raulin and Maillet, and informing himself each day of the observations they had gathered. His method was still combatted, and, while certain silk producers declared that it was excellent, certain organised bodies such as the Silk Commission of Lyons questioned its value. Pasteur forwarded to the members of this commission several samples of eggs, indicating in advance what result each of the samples should give. The boldness of his predictions was a proof of his certainty, and as a matter of fact they were realised. Nevertheless, his adversaries refused to lay down their arms, even though his processes began to be employed abroad, and the Austrian government awarded him a prize of ten thousand francs in recognition of the services he had rendered to the culture of silk-worms. Not only did Pasteur find a cure for *pébrine,* but also for another disease of silk-worms, known as *flacherie,* which was almost as much dreaded as the former.

Marechal Vaillant, Minister of the House to Napoleon III, decided to try the Pasteur method experimentally in one of the domains of the Crown. A vast property, planted with mulberry trees, was chosen. It belonged to the Prince Imperial, and was situated at Villa Vicentina, in Austrian Friuli. Pasteur set forth in November, 1869, with healthy eggs obtained by his process of cellular breeding from three cultivators, Messrs. Raybaud, Milhau and Gourdin; and immediately upon arriving he set to work. For the previous ten years the imperial domain, infected with pebrine and flacherie, had produced nothing, while the harvest resulting from Pasteur's eggs gave a net profit of twenty-two thousand francs. It formed a neat little surplus for the purse of the Prince Imperial.

Pasteur remained for eight months at Villa Vicentina, and there put the finishing touches to his work, in which he systematised all his previous studies on silkworms. His former master, Dumas, had the pleasure of introducing to the Academy of Sciences at a meeting held the 11th of April, 1870, and of pronouncing the eulogy on his *Studies on the Disease of Silkworms, a practical and assured Method of combatting it and preventing its Return.* The Academy had spoken, the victory was complete.

Pasteur had been made Senator of the Empire by a decree issued the previous July, and he was returning to France, impatient to begin new researches, when he learned at Strasburg, with an inexpressible sinking of the heart, that war had been declared. This meant the postponement of all his projects, of all those researches which he wished to undertake for the benefit of humanity. The scientists no longer had the floor!

[1] Cited by M. Valléry-Radot.

Chapter Five - The Spirit of Patriotism

PASTEUR was an ardent patriot, and the disasters of France affected him profoundly. Determined though he was to work, in spite of the war — since he had nothing else than his work to give to his country — it was, nevertheless, hard for him to reconcile himself, so keenly did he share the high tension of public feeling. Retiring to his boyhood home at Arbois, he sought to content himself with studying the fermentation of tan bark; yet all the while he was on the alert for news and quivering in unison with the soul of the nation at the announcement of each new defeat. When Paris was bombarded, and shells reached the Museum of Natural History, Chevreul's eloquent and indignant protest in the name of the Academy of Sciences caused Pasteur to regret that he had not been in Paris, in order to sign it, together with his colleagues who were present. But he remembered that in 1868 he had received a diploma from the University of Bonn, conferring upon him the honorary degree of Doctor of Medicine, in recognition of his brilliant work, and he decided to return it to the Dean. He accompanied it with a letter pulsating throughout with the highest kind of patriotism.

To Monsieur the Dean of the Faculty of Medicine at Bonn (Rhenish Prussia)

"Arbois, Jura, *January* 18th, 1871.

"Monsieur the Dean: In 1868 the Faculty of Medicine of the University of Bonn did me the honour to confer upon me voluntarily the degree of Doctor of Medicine, in recognition of my work in regard to fermentations and the role played by microscopic organisms. Among all the distinctions bestowed upon me by reason of the discoveries which I have been privileged to make since entering upon my scientific career, twenty-two years ago, there is none, i acknowledge, which caused me greater satisfaction. It was, in my eyes, the confirmation of a secret hope, of the truth of which I felt more and more convinced, namely, that my researches were opening up new horizons to the study of medicine.

"I even hastened to frame under glass that honorary degree which bore witness to the decision of your faculty, and I adorned the wall of my private office with it. Today the sight of this same parchment has become odious to me, and I feel that it is an insult to have my name, with the qualification of *virum clarissimum* which you bestowed upon it, placed under the auspices of a name condemned henceforth to the execration of my country, that of *rex Guilelmus.*

"While protesting loudly my profound respect towards you and all the other celebrated professors who signed their names at the foot of the document representing the decision of the members of your order, I must still obey the voice of my conscience and beg you to erase my name from the archives of your Faculty and to take back this diploma as a sign of the indignation aroused in a French savant by the barbarity and hypocrisy of the man who, for the sake of satisfying a criminal pride, obstinately insists upon the massacre of two great nations.

"Since the conference of Ferrières France has sought for the respect of human dignity, and Prussia for the triumph of the most abominable of lies, namely, that the future peace of Germany depends upon the dismemberment of France, although every sane man knows that the conquest of Alsace and Lorraine is simply a prize of war carried to the bitter end. Woe to the people of Germany if, being nearer than we to feudal servitude, they do not understand that France, while possessing the lands of Alsace and Lorraine, is not mistress of the consciences of their inhabitants. Savoy would still be a part of

Piedmont if its inhabitants had not consented, by a free vote, to become French. Such is the modern right of civilised nations, which your king is trampling under foot, and in defence of which France has risen.

"Therefore, there is perhaps no epoch of her history in which France has better deserved to be called the great nation, the initiator of progress, the guiding light of other races. Here is a whole people which has arisen against you, ready to push onward to the ends of the earth and to dare everything, because of her conviction of the justice and sanctity of her cause.

"Kindly accept. Monsieur the Dean, on behalf of yourself and your distinguished colleagues, the expression of my sentiments of high consideration.

"Louis Pasteur,
"Member of the Institute"

In the white heat of conflict between two powerful nations this reasonable and humane letter, couched in terms of such noble pride, could not be understood. Doctor Neumann, Dean of the Faculty of Bonn, replied harshly, with an affectation of disdain, under which he betrayed the irritation caused by this great and well-merited lesson. Pasteur, strong in the conviction that he and his nation were in the right, wrote a second letter, no longer indignant, but saddened and deploring the murderousness of war, which puts a barrier between men who were born to understand each other and to join forces in the search of happiness. He wrote:

"Monsieur the Dean: In re-reading your letter and my own, I feel sick at heart to think that men like you and myself, who have consecrated their lives to a search after the truth and to the progress of the human mind, could address each other in such terms, and based, for my own part, upon such acts. Nevertheless, we have there one other result of the character imprinted upon this war by your Emperor.

"You speak to me of degradation, Monsieur the Dean. There is degradation, be assured of that, and there will continue to be, down to the remotest epochs of time, attached to the memory of those who began the bombardment of Paris at a date when capitulation through famine was inevitable, and who continued this savage act when it had become evident to everyone that it would not hasten by a single hour the surrender of the heroic city,

"Louis Pasteur."

To the anguish of patriotism there were added private anxieties, for Pasteur's son, who was only eighteen years old, was serving as quartermaster in the Army of the East, under command of Bourbaki. Having been for a long time without news, Pasteur set out to seek for him among the demoralised troops in full retreat and destined finally to take refuge in Switzerland. He had the good fortune to find him in that disorganised crowd, emaciated, exhausted, but still living. After a few days of repose at Geneva, this son, well

41

worthy of his father, returned with him to France and reentered the service in the Army of National Defense.

International war was soon followed by civil war, and Pasteur, being unable either to enter Paris or to return to Arbois, which was occupied by the enemy, proceeded to install himself, early in 1871, in the house of his friend and collaborator, Émile Duclaux, who at that time was professor of chemistry in the Faculty of Clermont-Ferrand. He wrote to him on the 29th of March, 1871: "I have my head filled with the finest projects for work, but the war has forced my brain to lie fallow. I feel ready now to become productive again, although, alas, I may be deceiving myself! In any case I shall try. Ah, why am I not rich, a millionaire? I should then say to you, and to Raulin and Gernez and Van Tiegham, and the rest, 'Come! we are going to transform the world by our discoveries!' How fortunate you are to be young and in good health! Oh, if I could only recommence a new life of study and toil! Poor France! Dear mother land! If I could only contribute to relieve you from your disasters!"

At Clermont-Ferrand Pasteur hesitated between several paths. Should he continue to devote himself to silk-worms, or commence some new researches? Chance and the desire to do away with French consumption of an almost exclusive product of German industry turned his attention to the study of beer. Why should we not make good beer in France? Pasteur asked himself, and he straightway set to work to find an answer to his own question. There was a small brewery at Chamelieres, near Clermont, and it was there, at the home of the proprietor, M. Kulm, that he conducted his first experiments, afterwards verified in Duclaux's laboratory, in the Faculty of Sciences. The microscopic examination of malts, yeasts and beers soon convinced him that the latter acquired a bad taste through diseases analogous to those of wines, and due to certain microbes. In brewing, just as in all industries where fermentation plays the principal role, the manufacture was purely empirical, without method or science, and the results, whether good or bad, were often due to pure chance. Pasteur resolved to place brewing on a firm basis, established through experiments, to the end that it should yield nothing but perfect products.

Since beer was spoiled by the introduction of harmful germs, and its quality corresponded to the quality of the yeast which caused the fermentation, it was necessary, on the one hand, to eliminate germs, and, on the other, to obtain a thoroughly lively and perfectly pure yeast. These were the problems to which Pasteur applied himself, and during his sojourn at Clermont he manufactured beer according to his own rules, and was able to send a dozen bottles of it to Dumas!

But the brewery at Chamelières was too restricted a field. In September, 1871, he set out for England, and he reduced the great London brewers to a point of stupefaction by pronouncing upon the quality of their different beers, those that were good and those that were bad, simply by examining them under a microscope. With their practical temperament the English grasped the great benefit which their manufacture could derive from the method of the French scientist, and the microscope became a frequently consulted instrument in their breweries.

Upon returning to Paris, and once more installed in his laboratory at the École Normale, Pasteur still continued his studies of beer. The problem to be solved was a very delicate one. As a matter of fact, a beer may be good, even perfect, and yet be unpalatable, for the question of taste intervenes, quite aside from the quality of the manufacture.

"Now, for the purpose of carrying on this work of adaptation and of detail," writes M. Duclaux, "Pasteur had none of the essential requisites. He did not like beer, and, although by force of will, he succeeded in acquiring a sufficiently trained palate and sense of taste, he remained unable to detect differences pointed out by the brewers themselves, and which he was sometimes amazed to find keenly appreciated by his friend Bertin, who lived next to him in the École Normale (as assistant director), and who was frequently invited into the laboratory for conferences over the relative flavour of samples. In the face of the enthusiastic appreciations sometimes expressed by his friend, Pasteur remained bewildered, feeling that they were leading him into regions where he did not like to venture, and he would forthwith have renounced this labour of Sisyphus, if he had not had the imprudence to solicit the pecuniary aid of a certain society for investigations, a very large and generous society, towards which he had thus contracted a moral obligation to succeed in his enterprise.

In order to arrive at the conclusion which he wished the laboratory did not suffice his needs. Accordingly, Pasteur went to continue his researches at the great breweries belonging to the Tourtel brothers at Tantonville. Above all else, he recommended the most scrupulous cleanliness in all the manipulations and all the implements of manufacture.

Let us here introduce a parenthesis for the purpose of pointing out the extent to which Pasteur insisted upon cleanliness in all the details of daily life. He never seated himself at table without carefully wiping his plates, his glass, his knife and fork, examining them all with the most severe attention. He never ate fruit that was not peeled, and he even scraped off the crust from his bread, for fear that it might be infected with microbes. These habits were well known to his family, but they could not have failed to astonish his hostesses when he dined away from home.

After a short sojourn at the Tourtel Brothers' brewery, in company with his assistant, M. Grenet, Pasteur announced that all the diseases of beer arose from microbes which could be avoided through precautions in the course of manufacture, that it was necessary to make careful selection of yeasts, and that, if bottled beer was heated to the point of 122 degrees Fahrenheit, it was rendered unalterable.

ÉMILE DUCLAUX (after BORDES) - The favorite disciple of the great scientist and the first director of the Institute in the Rue Dutot, who collaborated in Pasteur's researches and carried on his work.

His method and his processes have enabled France to cope successfully with foreign competition, and the congress of French brewers, held in 1889, attributed all the merit of their products to his labours.

After the close of the war the world of science so highly appreciated the genius of Pasteur that the celebrated Englishman, Huxley, did not hesitate to declare that his discoveries were worth the five billion ransom of France. And yet this was only the first part of his work, the part which, according to Duclaux, had won him fame, while now he was about to enter upon the second part — devoted to human maladies — which was destined to assure him immortality.

Chapter Six - The Curative Poison

INNOVATORS, whether in the arts or the sciences, are combatted at the outset. Pasteur was not destined to escape the general rule, which demands that all truth shall be forced upon us. In spite of the evidence which he had obtained in support of his theories from long and difficult experiments with fermentations, a group of scientists, and they by no means the lesser lights, refused to accept his conclusions. Pie had to face a controversy with Trécul, who maintained that microscopic organisms could transform themselves, one into another, and he must needs demonstrate that, contrary to this opinion, they remained fixed and with a specific character. In the course of the study necessitated by this discussion he made experiments on *anaërobic* (without air) and *aërobic* (with air) forms of life, and he discovered that a certain number of these organisms could pass from one mode of life to the other with an accompanying change in form and function.

But these studies of fermentations, through which he was destined to refute Claude Bernard, Berthelot, etc., studies which he pursued with unflagging energy, and which were shedding light upon phenomena that had remained obscure until he had given the key to their interpretation, did not prevent him from pondering over the role played by microbes in infectious diseases or from beginning experiments concerning them.

Pasteur had been elected to full membership of the Academy of Medicine in 1873, and it was thenceforward there that he waged his battles against prejudice, hostility and unfairness, in order to achieve the triumph of ideas which brought with them the most complete revolution that had ever taken place in medicine. Along the curve of an inspired path, and with no break in the continuity, he had passed from crystals to fermentations, and from fermentations to diseases of microbic origin. But these divisions are still in a measure inexact, for, within his vast brain that was forever working all his projects for experimentation, all his ideas centred upon germs. Accordingly he was able to say before the Academy of Medicine in 1873: "Is it not evident that all the researches to which I have devoted myself for seventeen years, regardless of the efforts they have cost me, are the products of the same ideas, the same principles, forced by incessant toil to yield constantly new results? The best proof that an investigator is on the road to truth is the uninterrupted fertility of his labours."

For years Pasteur was forced to fight his battles in the very midst of the Academy of Medicine, and he did so with a vigorous and dogged energy so long as he was defending the truth contained in his discoveries. His work, for that matter, controverted though it was, had long since passed beyond the limits of scientific circles, and in 1874 the National Assembly, wishing to pay honour to his rare merit, awarded him a national recompense, one which had been granted only twice before within the century, in 1839 to Daguerre and Niepce, and in 1845 to the engineer Vicat. Paul Bert was appointed to make the report. In the course of it he said: "The discoveries of M. Pasteur, after having shed new light upon the obscure question of fermentations and of the mode in which microscopic organisms make their appearance, have revolutionised certain branches of business industry, agriculture and pathology. One is struck with admiration when one realises that so many results and such widely different ones have all been derived, through an unbroken chain of facts, followed up step by step, leaving nothing to conjecture, from an original theoretical study as to the manner in which tartaric acid deflects polarised light. Never before has that famous epigram, 'Genius is patience,' received so splendid a confirmation.

"It is this admirable combination of theoretical and practical work which the Government proposes that you should honour with a national recompense. Your Committee unanimously approves this proposition.

"The recompense specified consists of a life pension of twelve thousand francs; this sum represents very nearly the salary attached to the professorship in the Sorbonne, from which illness has obliged M. Pasteur to resign."

In this same report Paul Bert paid tribute to the disinterestedness of Pasteur^ whose discoveries had enriched France to the extent of unnumbered millions, without its having occurred to him to acquire any personal benefit from them. The motion was carried by 532 affirmative votes against 24 negative ones. It was an overwhelming majority.

Having once turned his attention to infectious diseases, Pasteur assiduously frequented the Academy of Medicine. Becoming convinced that the majority of deaths were caused by wounds coming in contact with external germs, he recommended to the operating surgeons a method of antiseptic dressing, based upon his discovery of microbes in the air. The great English surgeon, Lister, employed a similar method, and obtained excellent results. The French physicians who accepted Pasteur's method saw the percentage of deaths resulting from operations fall off with great rapidity. It was not adopted without opposition, but its efficacy was soon recognised; and to-day there is no surgeon who does not follow out all of Pasteur's careful injunctions, the heating of instruments, the sterilisation of dressings, antiseptic washing of the wound, etc.

It was in 1876 that science escaped a real danger. Pasteur, yielding to the solicitations of a number of electors, presented himself as candidate at the election of senators from the Jura. He made his electoral campaign with the same seriousness that he displayed in his laboratory, proclaiming in his sign bills and circulars that his only reason for wishing to be elected was that he might have further opportunity to serve France. M. Grévy presented himself in opposition at Lons-le-Saulnier, and Pasteur received only 62 votes. He cherished no grudge because of this defeat, but he declared that his incursion into the domain of politics had been a mistake, and he promptly returned to his studies.

He had, for that matter, quite enough to do in defending his own scientific work, which had been newly attacked just as he began to believe that it had been definitely established. Bastian, for instance, despite the convincing nature of his experiments on spontaneous generation, disputed his results, and Pasteur, though he might well have rested on his earlier labours, repeated them, if possible with even greater care, in order to be able to answer him. This experimental method, this close scrutiny of facts which formed the basis of all Pasteur's discoveries, this constant anxiety to leave nothing doubtful or unfinished, has lately been testified to by M. Denys Cochin, a member of the Académie Française and a deputy, on the occasion of the discussion before the Chamber in regard to powder for the navy. 'I have studied chemistry to some extent,' he said, 'and I recall a remark once made to me by one of our most illustrious scientists. I had finished some small research, the report on which I submitted to M. Pasteur. It began with a phrase that is common enough in manuals of chemistry: 'We know that...' 'What do we know?' Pasteur said to me, 'We know nothing at all.'

"I replied, 'Excuse me, Monsieur, but the fact I cited was taken from one of your own writings.' I thought I had the best of it, but Pasteur merely rejoined, 'That has nothing to do with it; you ought to have verified me.'"

Therein lies Pasteur's whole secret: he always repeated his experiments over and over until he was certain of the truths that they contained; and it was by this means that he triumphed over his adversaries. His controversy with Bastian, together with a posthumous paper by Claude Bernard on fermentations, led him to investigate the fermentation of grapes. Having constructed a hot-house on a small property that he owned near Arbois, Pasteur succeeded in demonstrating that the fermentation was due exclusively to germs which made their appearance on the surface of the grapes and on the bark of the vines at the moment of maturity, and that neither verjuice nor the must of the grape isolated from the skins and stems can undergo fermentation.

But, although he was still disputed, he had the keen pleasure of seeing certain of his methods eagerly adopted by the big industries. During a visit to a vast Italian silk-worm establishment, on the occasion of a congress of silk producers held at Milan, he beheld his own name inscribed across the pediment of the building, in conspicuous homage to the services he had rendered to that industry. On this same occasion they showed him the marvellous results obtained by his process of cellular culture, practically carried out by young girls who had acquired great expertness in the use of the microscope for detecting corpusculous moths.

As in the case of the fermentation of grapes, this was a side issue of his theory of germs, but at this epoch he was studying them mainly from the pathological point of view, and we know that he was interested above all in diseases of a microbic origin. There again he was destined to wage stout battles against routine and prejudice, even within the walls of the Academy of Medicine.

It was the disease of anthrax, which annually decimated the herds and flocks of France, that Pasteur chose as the first point of attack. Davaine had previously discovered that the blood of animals infected with this disease contained little rectilinear, stick-like organisms, a species of vibrion which he named from their form *bacterides,* and which were the cause of the disease: but he had been unable to defend his conclusions against Messrs. Gaillard and Leplat, professors at Val-de-Grace, and Paul Bert, who all maintained, after making experiments, that anthrax came from a virus, and not from the *bacterides* themselves. It was precisely at this point in the discussion, with the two sides steadfastly maintaining contradictory opinions, each supported equally by facts, that Pasteur, in collaboration with Messrs. Joubert, Chamberland and Roux, intervened in his accustomed manner, quite simple, quite clear and rigorously scientific.

Having obtained a fresh drop of blood from an animal infected with anthrax, Pasteur cultivated the *bacterides* in artificial mediums by impregnating each new medium with a drop taken from the preceding culture, so that by the time of the tenth culture he obtained pure *bacterides.* When these were used for inoculation they produced anthrax, without the aid of the original drop of blood, which had disappeared through being diluted to such a degree as to be imperceptible in the later cultures. This amounted to a complete confirmation of Davaine's opinion, that these *bacterides* were the cause of the disease of anthrax. In order to render his experiment more decisive Pasteur established a counter-proof by inoculating his medium with a culture from which he had eliminated the bacterides by means of filtering it through plaster, and the resulting liquid failed to produce anthrax.

Pursuing his studies further, he demonstrated that Messrs. Gaillard and Leplat, who asserted that they had produced anthrax in animals by means of blood which contained no *bacterides*, had been mistaken, and that what they had really done was to produce a different disease by inoculating with a new species of microbe, which he named the *septic vibrion.* In like manner he refuted Paul Bert, who, after having destroyed the bacteria of anthrax by

48

means of compressed oxygen, claimed that the blood thus deprived of them could nevertheless cause anthrax; Pasteur showed that this blood still contained the germs or spores of *bacterides,* which had greater resistant powers than the *bacterides* themselves, and that it was from them that these cases of anthrax came, so that in any case it was caused either by the *bacterides* or by their spores. This amounted to a definite proof of the parasitic character of this infectious disease.

But how was anthrax communicated to animals, and was there any hope of protecting them from it? Again, as in the case of the silkworms, the Minister of Agriculture commissioned Pasteur to make a study of this evil, which ravaged the cattle-raising districts, causing losses which amounted annually to tens of millions. Nothing was known beyond the fact that the animals who were pastured in certain fields that were known as *bad fields* became infected with anthrax. Pasteur installed himself in the environs of Chartres and began his researches. He was accompanied by M. Roux, who bears witness to the perspicacity of his observations conducted on the spot:

"The harvest had been gathered," he wrote, "and nothing remained but the stubble. Pasteur's attention was drawn to a certain portion of the field, because of the different colouring of the earth. The owner explained that this was the spot where they had buried the sheep which had died of anthrax the preceding year. Pasteur, who always examined things closely, noticed on the surface of the soil a multitude of little lumps of earth thrown up by earthworms. The idea then occurred to him that in their continuous journeyings from the lower depths to the surface the worms carried above ground some of the soil rich in the humus that surrounded the dead bodies, and along with it some of the spores of anthrax which it contained. But Pasteur never stopped short at conjectures. He immediately passed on to experiments. These justified his expectations: the earth contained in one of the worms, when used to inoculate guinea-pigs, produced anthrax in them." (Roux, *L'oeuvre médicale de Pasteur,* Agenda du Chimiste, 1896.)

Pasteur had studied first the active cause of the disease, and next its mode of propagation, and found that the spores penetrated into the organism of the animals, sheep or cattle, through the mucous membranes of their mouths, where they were torn by the dry and prickly grass. How were the flocks and herds to be preserved? It was through his study of chicken cholera, carried on simultaneously with that of anthrax, that he was set upon the right path. He had noticed that the cholera microbes (at this time the word *microbe,* as a generic term for *vibrions, bacterides,* etc., had just been coined by Sedillot, a surgeon at Strasburg, approved by Littre, and generally adopted by scientists), if left exposed to the air, and then used for a new culture, lost their virulence to the point of becoming actually harmless. This attenuation was due to the oxygen in the air. This discovery was destined to revolutionise the science of medicine, and to lead Pasteur to the employment of vaccines, which he obtained after several years of extremely delicate experiments.

It was on the 28th of February, 1881, that Pasteur made his communication to the Academy of Sciences regarding the vaccine of anthrax. It was received by some with enthusiasm, and by others with mistrust. Pasteur himself was certain of the effects of his discovery, healthy animals inoculated with the attenuated virus would surely be rendered immune to anthrax. He consented to make a test on a large scale, and this test justly remained celebrated. It began on the 5th of May, 1881, on a farm at Pouilly-le-Fort, near Melun, under the auspices of the Society of Agriculture of that town. The conditions imposed were most rigorous, but Pasteur was confident of victory. Fifty sheep and ten cows were turned over to him: of the former lot twenty-five were to be vaccinated with an attenuated virus and then to receive, together with the other twenty-five which had not been vaccinated, an inoculation of extremely virulent anthrax microbes; while for the second lot the experiment was to be tried upon six vaccinated animals and four not vaccinated. Pasteur asserted that all those which had been vaccinated would resist the disease of anthrax, while those which had not been vaccinated would all die. This claim had the audacity of genius, and throughout the duration of the experiments the illustrious scientist underwent alternations of joyous hope and feverish anxiety. But on the 2d of June, the day fixed by Pasteur for judging the results, after the inoculation with virulent *bacterides,* which took place on May 31, it proved to be a triumphant occasion for him on the farm at Pouilly-le-Fort. The prefect of Seine-et-Marne, several deputies and senators, veterinaries and journalists were present, all quivering with impatience — and Pasteur's predictions were realised in every particular amid the congratulations of an enthusiastic throng. Every one of the animals which had been inoculated but not vaccinated had contracted anthrax and died, while all the animals that had been both inoculated and vaccinated escaped all symptoms of illness.

On the 13th of June Pasteur communicated to the Academy of Sciences the result of his experiments at Pouilly-le-Fort, which was henceforth to be known as "The Pasteur Farm." In view of their success, which had made an enormous sensation, he was able to say:

"We now possess virus-vaccines against anthrax, capable of warding off the deadly disease, without ever proving fatal themselves — living vaccines, that may be cultivated at will and transported anywhere without suffering harm; vaccines, in short, that are prepared by a method which we have reason to believe is susceptible of being generalised, because it has once already been put into practice for the purpose of obtaining vaccine against chicken cholera. Because of the character of the conditions which I have here enumerated, and looking at the question only from the scientific point of view, I may say that the discovery of vaccine for anthrax constitutes a perceptible progress in advance of Jenner's vaccine, because the latter was not obtained as a result of experiments."

Pasteur no longer met with the same obstacles that had confronted his method for the culture of silk-worms; his vaccines for anthrax were in demand in every cattle-raising district of France. Within one year after the above-mentioned experiments the number of animals vaccinated had risen to 613,740 sheep and 83,946 cattle!

But before this triumph — which had even been questioned in certain circles — he had to answer numerous criticisms at the Academy of Medicine, where too many of the "dear masters" refused to recognise him as anything more than a chemist. He was forced to fight on behalf of his germ theory against the adherents of the old school who refused to accept not only the novelty of the theory, but even the very existence of germs. He was forced to defend his experiments when they were called in question, and one day he actually brought some chickens into a meeting at the Academy of Medicine, in order to convince Colin that he could infect them with anthrax! Pasteur was an energetic adversary, and sometimes a violent one, if anyone affected not to understand him; and he defended what he believed to be the truth with crude and caustic eloquence. It very nearly led him into a duel with Jules Guerin in October, 1881, because of his rather rough treatment of him on the subject of smallpox.

This whole epoch of Pasteur's life, extending from 1877 to 1882, was extremely prolific. He was possessed by what amounted to a fever for work, and his ideas radiated in all directions. His laboratory was a veritable hive. Together with his anthrax vaccine, he found that of chicken cholera; and his pupil, Thuillier, discovered the microbe of *rouget* in swine. But in the midst of all his polemics and his divers other duties Pasteur's chief preoccupation was that of human diseases. He turned his attention to puerperal fever, and, having demonstrated that it was due to a microbe, he outlined for doctors a whole series of measures of precaution and cleanliness that were destined to save many a mother. He collected notes on the plague, he made a study of boils, he haunted the hospitals in company of his students, notwithstanding his sensitiveness and physical repugnance.

"The sight of corpses, the sad necessity of autopsies caused him actual repulsion," writes M. Roux. "How many times we have seen him hastily leave the amphitheatre of the hospitals because he was actually ill! But his love of science, his curiosity to know the truth were even stronger; he always came back on the morrow."

After having conquered himself in order to bring to humanity effective remedies against infectious diseases, Pasteur was destined to conquer the doctors themselves, bound though they were to the old formulas, the antiquated conceptions, and who could not, without some vexation and alarm, behold the overthrow of their tranquillity and peaceful routine.

But the excitement aroused by the discovery of anthrax vaccine, which opened such great hopes for the future, was confirmed by the learned societies and the ruling powers. The Society of the Agriculturists of France awarded Pasteur, on the 21st of February, 1881, a medal of honour, and the Government bestowed upon him the *grand cordon* of the Legion of Honour. In this connection we meet with a typical manifestation of Pasteur's character. He sent word that he would not accept this elevation to a higher rank unless his two collaborators, Chamberland and Roux, were each to receive the red ribbon.

Chapter Seven - The Sovereignty of Genius

IN spite of a small refractory group, Pasteur's rise into fame was continuous, and his genius radiated throughout the scientific world of Europe. The government had appointed him as delegate to the International Medical Congress held at London in April, 1881; and there he was the recipient of exceptional honours. M. Vallery-Radot cites a very beautiful letter, which Pasteur wrote to his wife concerning the attentions that he received. When the President of the Congress; Sir James Paget, happened to mention his name, the entire assemblage burst into applause, and Pasteur was obliged to rise and salute his colleagues.

"I was very proud," he wrote, "very proud internally, not for myself — you know how I feel in regard to triumphs — but for my country, when I realised that I was being exceptionally distinguished in the midst of this immense concourse of foreigners, of Germans especially, who are here in considerable numbers, far greater numbers than there are Frenchmen, of whom nevertheless, taken altogether, there are not less than two hundred and fifty. Jean Baptiste and René were present at the session. You can judge of their emotion.

"After the session, luncheon at the home of Sir James Paget, with the Prussian Prince seated on his right and the Prince of Wales on his left. Then a gathering of twenty-five to thirty guests in the drawing-room. Sir James presented me to the Prince of Wales, before whom I made my bow, telling him that I was happy to salute the friend of France.

"'Yes,' he answered me, 'a great friend.'

"Sir James Paget had the good taste not to ask me to be presented to the Prussian Prince. Although under such circumstances it was impossible to be otherwise than courteous, I could not have made up my mind to give the appearance of having asked to be presented to him. But all of a sudden the Prince himself came up to me and said:

"'Monsieur Pasteur, allow me to introduce myself to you, and to tell you that I was one of those who applauded you this morning.' And he continued talking to me in the friendliest manner."

Receptions and ceremonies did not make Pasteur forget his serious work; and in a lecture intended as an answer to Bastian, who maintained that germs were born from the organism containing them, he described his labours, his methods, his discovery of vaccines, and the way in which he had proved experimentally that germs were parasites. This exposition by Pasteur, in which he summed up his entire life as a scientist, and all the opportunities which it had opened up to the future of science, was printed in English and sent to all the members of the House of Commons. The greatest English scientists, it should be added, Tyndall, Paget and Lister, had rallied to the support of the Pasteur methods.

Upon returning to France, he set forth immediately for Bordeaux, where he hoped to have a chance to study yellow fever, which had broken out among the crew of the *Condé*, just arrived from Senegal. Yet, at the same time that he was anxiously concerned regarding these sick sailors, among whom he hoped to find subjects for experiments, he was profiting by his leisure moments to visit the Bordeaux library, where he read the works of Littré assiduously, and with pen in hand. The fact was that certain members of the Académie Française had asked Pasteur to present himself as candidate for the place of the learned linguist, then recently deceased.

We have seen that Pasteur, the great revolutionist of science, had a deep respect for degrees, hierarchies, social orders and honorary distinctions, and it seemed to him that this was an honour out of all proportion to his own literary claims. He hesitated, and it needed all the insistence of his friends, as well as the thought that it was a tribute paid to science rather than to him personally, to decide him to offer himself as a candidate. He was elected on December 8th, 1881, to the thirty-first chair, whose previous occupants had been De La Chambre (1635), Desmarais (1670), LaMonnoye (1713), La Riviere (1727), Hardion (1730), Thomas (1766), Guilbert (1786), Fontanes (1803), Villemain (1821), and Littre (1881). It may well be said that, even though he was not a man of letters, Pasteur's name will remain as the one which has shed the greatest lustre upon that particular chair.

His reception took place on the 27th of April, 1882, and it was the philosopher, Ernest Renan, who as master of ceremonies, welcomed the scientist. Their two addresses, each in its respective form and spirit, are admirable monuments of the French language and of French thought. That of Pasteur, grave, austere, profound, paying homage to the merit of Littré, opening up marvellous glimpses into the abysses of infinity; that of Renan, respectful towards science, complimentary, witty and permeated with a serene and subtle philosophy.

Louis Pasteur was listened to with a religious attention, and something like a shiver passed over his hearers when he read, in a voice which, while not strong, was animated by an ardent conviction, this celebrated passage:

"Above and beyond the starry vault, what is there? Other new star-lit skies. So be it! And above and beyond them? The human mind, urged on by an invincible force, will never cease to ask itself. What is there beyond? What if the mind should try to stop at some point, either in time or space? Since that point where it stops marks only a finite greatness, merely greater than those which preceded it, the mind has scarcely begun to contemplate it when the implacable question returns, and never can its curiosity be silenced. It does no good to answer. Above and beyond, are space, time, greatness without limit. No one comprehends these words. Whoever proclaims the existence of the infinite, and no one can evade doing so, sums up in that affirmation more of the supernatural than is contained in all the miracles of all religions; for the notion of the infinite has this double character, of being undeniable and incomprehensible. When this notion once takes possession of our understanding there is nothing left but to prostrate ourselves before it. More than that, at this moment of poignant anguish, we must needs crave mercy from our own brains; all the sources of intellectual life threaten to give way; we feel ourselves on the point of yielding to the sublime folly of Pascal. This positive and primordial notion is gladly set aside, with all its consequences, by modern positivism, in the social life of today.

"On all sides I find the inevitable expression of this idea of the infinite in our world. It is through this that the supernatural lies at the bottom of every heart. The idea of God is one form of the idea of the infinite. So long as the mystery of the infinite weighs upon human thought, temples will be raised to the cult of the infinite, whether God be called Brahma, Allah, Jehovah or Jesus. And on the pavement of these temples we will see men kneeling, prostrated, lost in the thought of the infinite. Metaphysics does nothing more than transfer to within ourselves this dominant notion of the infinite. And is not the conception of the ideal merely a faculty reflected from the infinite, which leads us, when in the presence of beauty, to conceive of a still higher form of beauty? Are science and the passionate desire to understand anything else than the effect of that spur towards knowledge which the mystery of the universe has placed in our souls? Where are the true sources of human dignity, of liberty, of modern democracy, unless they are contained in the idea of the infinite, before which all men are equal?"

His hearers had applauded the words of the scientist who had thus dizzily scrutinised the mysteries of the world; they were about to hear the phrases of the philosopher, who was pondering them with a smile. Ernest Renan welcomed Pasteur with words of graceful compliment and noble distinction:

"We are quite incompetent to bestow fitting praise upon that which constitutes your true glory," he said, "those admirable experiments through which you attain the very confines of life, your ingenious fashion of interrogating nature, which so many times has won from her the clearest kind of replies, those precious discoveries which, day by day, are being transformed into conquests of the highest importance to humanity. You would repudiate our praises, habituated as you are to value only the judgments of your peers; and in the scientific debates, aroused by this host of new ideas, you would not care to see the appreciations of men of letters intruding among the acclaims of scientists related to you by the brotherhood of glory and toil. Between you and your rival scientists we have no right to intervene. But, apart from the basis of science, which is not our province, there is one criterion, Monsieur, in regard to which our knowledge of the human mind gives us the right to express an opinion. There is something which we are able to recognise in its most diverse manifestations, something which belongs in equal degree to Galileo, to Pascal, to Michelangelo and to Moliere; something which constitutes the sublimity of the poet, the profundity of the philosopher, the fascination of the orator, the divination of the savant. This common basis of all beautiful and true works, this divine flame, this indefinable breath which is the inspiration of science, literature and art, we find in you. Monsieur: it is genius. No one else has traversed with so assured a step the circles of elemental nature; your scientific life is like a luminous trail across the great night of the infinitely small, in those furthest depths of being, where life is born."

After analysing the work of Pasteur, and pointing out the strong continuity of his researches, Renan spoke of his virtues.

"Your austere life," he said, "wholly consecrated to disinterested research, is the best response to those who regard our century as having lost the heritage of the great gifts of the soul. Your laborious assiduity has been a stranger to all recreation and repose."

Then, having recognised the merits of Littré, Renan concluded, with rare and exquisite subtlety:

^'Your absolute devotion to science gave you the right. Monsieur, to succeed to such a man and to recall to us his great and revered memory. You will find in our meetings a source of relaxation for your mind continually occupied with new discoveries. This association with a company composed of all sorts of opinions and every type of mind will be congenial to you; here we have the pleasant laugh of comedy, the pure and tender romance, the soaring flight of poetry, with its harmonious rhythm; there we have all the subtlety of moral observation, the most exquisite analysis of the works of the mind, the profound significance of history. None of this will shake your faith in your experiments; the right acid will remain the right acid, the left acid will remain the left acid. But you will find that the prudent labours of M. Littré also had their value. You will follow with some interest the care taken by our critical philosophy to eliminate error, by mistrusting its own procedure and limiting the extent of its observations. When you see how many good things are taught by those branches of letters that are frivolous in appearance, you will come to believe that the discreet doubt, the smile, the fine play of wit of which Pascal speaks, also have their value. Among us you will find no experiments to make; but that modest power of observation, from which you demand so much, will suffice to procure you many a pleasant hour. We will communicate our hesitations to you: and you will communicate your assurance to us. You will bring us, above all, your glory, your genius, and the renown of your discoveries. Monsieur, I bid you welcome."

Pasteur was succeeded in the Académie Française by Gaston Paris, the restorer of the old national literature of France; and on the occasion of his reception the illustrious scientist, J. Bertrand, who responded to his address, told some delicious anecdotes of Pasteur, his works and his character.

"Already illustrious," he said, "but not yet celebrated, Pasteur was appointed to express, before the statue of Thenard, the homage of the École Normale. He was scheduled to speak among the very last of the orators. When he arose to make his address the crowd, weary of eloquence, continued to applaud, but had ceased to listen. Without wasting time by relating for the fifteenth occasion trivial anecdotes and doubtful legends, without even mentioning hydrogen peroxide, Pasteur paid Thénard the admirable tribute of dwelling only on his kindliness, recalling only his sense of justice. From the opening words his earnest and effective phrases penetrated to the very heart, and, while even the remotest hearers followed him with close attention, tears of emotion filled the eyes of all. Occasions such as that were rare.

It was only when he was forced to it that Pasteur showed the brilliance of his mind. One day at the Academy of Sciences two contradictory spirits were raising objections unworthy of attention regarding certain discoveries. After a crushing reply, Pasteur, apostrophising them both together, said to the one, 'Do you know what you lack? You lack the power of observation!' and to the other, 'And you, the power of reasoning!' A murmur arose. The Academy was protesting against the lack of courtesy in his form of speech. Pasteur at once interrupted himself.

"The heat of the discussion carried me away,' he said; 'I regret my impetuosity. I beg that my colleagues will accept my sincere apology.'

"His extreme simplicity and frankness pleased the members, when suddenly he added:

"I have acknowledged myself at fault; I have willingly made my excuses; may I not be permitted to plead an extenuating circumstance? It is this, that what I said was true!'

"And, after a moment's reflection, he added:

"'Absolutely true!'

"A unanimous and appreciative laugh enlivened the Academy, and, like sensible persons, his two adversaries joined in."

In accordance with Renan's expressed desire, Pasteur frequently attended the meetings of the Academie Française. He sometimes went there in the company of M. Duruy, the Minister of Public Instruction, who had encouraged his early efforts, for it happened that one of them lived at the École Normale, in the Rue d'Ulm, and the other in the Rue de Médicis. One Thursday, when they had taken a modest fiacre to drive to the Institute, it happened to be Duruy who, upon arriving at their destination, tendered a five-franc piece to the coachman.

"No change," said the latter.

"Then keep the whole piece in memory of the occasion; you have driven the leading scientist of the century."

Pasteur immediately put his hand in his pocket, drew out a brand-new crown, and said:

"Here, my friend, take this also, because you have driven the greatest minister of the Second Empire!"

The coachman looked somewhat bewildered, but eminently happy, while the two academicians entered the court of the Palais Mazarin, still laughing.

For Pasteur, one homage succeeded another. The town of Aubenas, saved from ruin by his discoveries in regard to the disease of silkworms, presented him, in May, 1882, with a work of art in which the microscope was portrayed as rendering possible the cultivation of healthy silk-worms. Next it was Nimes which awarded him a medal for his vaccine against anthrax; and next Montpellier, where the Agricultural Society organised a solemn meeting for the purpose of thanking him for having vanquished anthrax, and to beg him to cure the rot and the phylloxera. He had become the great magician.

But he had against him certain "beloved brethren" who, either in good faith or otherwise, combatted the doctrine of microbes, and he had to sustain some hard contests against the doubting Peters of the Academy of Medicine. On the other hand, the German school, with Dr. Koch at its head, disputed his discoveries, going so far as to deny wholly the value of his observations. But he was so certain of the positive results he had obtained that he sent his pupil Thuillier as a delegate to Germany, with virulent cultures of anthrax, as well as attenuated viruses, thus carrying his experiments into the territory of the enemy.

He suffered from such ill will, and from all these quarrels, ceaselessly renewed; his resentment, however, was softened by the admiration he received from the great majority of scientists. The Academy of Sciences having taken the initiative, the learned societies subscribed towards a medal to be presented to him, containing his profile modeled by Alphée Dubois, with this inscription: "To Louis Pasteur, from his colleagues, his friends and his admirers." This token was presented to him on the 25th of January, 1882, and Pasteur had the pleasure of seeing his old teacher, Dumas, heading the delegation, which consisted of Boussingault, Bouley, Jamin, Daubrée, Bertin, Tisserand, and Davaine, and of hearing him deliver the presentation speech — Dumas, whom as an obscure youth he had listened to at the Sorbonne, leaving the lecture room moved to the point of tears.

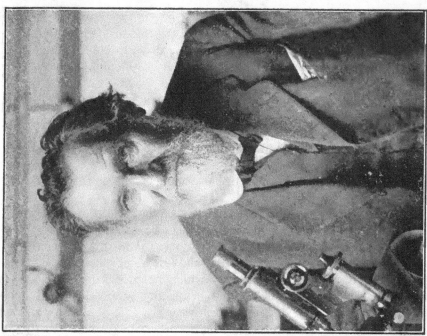

TWO OF PASTEUR'S GREAT COLLABORATORS - *Left:* Doctor Roux, director
of the Pasteur Institute, and inventor of the method of treating diphtheria by
a serum obtained from horses. *Right:* Doctor Metchnikoff, celebrated for his
theory of phagocytosis and his works on the intestinal flora.

The Government did not remain insensible to the enthusiastic movement in recognition of the discoveries of Pasteur. Upon the second report by Paul Bert, the French Chambers raised Pasteur's pension to 25,000 francs, in imitation of Germany, which had accorded Jenner 250,000 francs in 1802 and 500,000 in 1807 for his vaccine against small-pox. Paul Bert's report summed up Pasteur's works as follows:

"They can be classed," he wrote, "in three series; they constitute three great discoveries:

"The first may be formulated as follows: *Each fermentation is the product of the development of a special microbe.*

"The second may be formulated: *Each infectious disease* (or at least those which have been studied by M. Pasteur or his immediate disciples) *is produced by the development of some special microbe within the organism.*

'The third may be expressed as follows: *The microbe of an infectious disease, if cultivated under certain specified conditions, becomes attenuated in respect to its harmful qualities; it has been converted from a virus into a vaccine.*

"As practical consequences of the first discovery, M. Pasteur has given rules for the manufacture of vinegar and beer, and he has shown how beer and wine may be preserved from those secondary fermentations which turn them sour, cause *l'amer, la graisse, la pousse,* and prevent their transportation and often even their preservation on the spot where they are produced.

"As practical consequences of the second discovery, M. Pasteur has prescribed the rules to be followed in order to protect our flocks and herds from the contamination of anthrax and our silk-worms from the maladies which destroy them. On the other hand, our surgeons have, succeeded under its guidance in almost completely doing away with erysipelas and other purulent infections which formerly caused the death of so many patients after operations.

"As practical consequences of the third discovery, M. Pasteur has prescribed the rules to be followed in order to save the horses, cattle and sheep, and, in point of fact, has saved them from the disease of anthrax, which annually caused their death in France, to the value of twenty million francs. Swine also are now protected from *rouget,* which decimated them, and the barn-door fowl, from the chicken cholera, which caused terrible ravages among them. And now there is every reason to hope that hydrophobia also will soon be conquered."

The motion calling for an increase of the national recompense was passed unanimously, but a ceremony even dearer to Pasteur's heart than this grateful homage of an entire people was in preparation in the little town of his birth. On the 14th of July, 1883, a commemorative tablet was placed upon the house in which Pasteur was born, and M. Kaempfen, director of the Beaux-Arts, who had been delegated by the Government, said at its inauguration:

"In the name of the Government of the Republic, I salute this inscription, which recalls the fact that on the 27th of December, 1822, there was born in this little street one who was destined to become one of the greatest scientists of a century, whose greatness lies in science, and one who by his admirable labours has augmented the glory of his native land and won the gratitude of all humanity."

Pasteur spoke in reply, and his address reveals the great qualities of his generous heart, his extreme personal modesty, and the pride which he cherished on behalf of science alone.

"Gentlemen," he said, "I am deeply moved by the honour done me by the town of Dôle; but permit me, while expressing my appreciation, to utter a protest against this excess of glory. In according me a homage which is rendered only to the illustrious dead, you are usurping in advance the judgment of posterity.

"Will posterity ratify your decision, and ought you not, Monsieur the Mayor, have prudently advised the municipal council not to pass such a hasty resolution?

"But having made my protest, gentlemen, against this public proof of an admiration which I do not deserve, allow me to say that I am touched and moved to the bottom of my soul. Your sympathetic tribute has united in this commemorative tablet the two great things which have formed at once the passion and the charm of my life: my love of science and my attachment to the paternal hearth.

"Oh! my father and my mother! oh! my dear lost ones, who lived so modestly in this little house, it is you to whom I owe everything! Your enthusiasm, my valiant mother, you passed on to me. If I have always associated the greatness of science with the greatness of my native land, it is because I was impregnated with the sentiments which you inspired in me. And you, my dear father, whose life was as hard as your own hard craft, it is you who taught me what can be done by patience and long effort. It is you to whom I owe tenacious persistence in the daily task. Not only did you have those qualities of perseverance which result in useful lives, but you also had admiration for great men and great deeds. To aim higher and higher, to learn more and more, to seek constantly to rise, such were the things you taught me. I can still see you, at the close of your laborious day, reading in the evening the account of some battle from one of the volumes of contemporaneous history which recalled to your mind the glorious epoch of which you had been witness. While teaching me to read, you also took pains to teach me the greatness of France.

"My blessings on you both, my dear parents, for all that you have been, and let me pass on to you the homage that has today been paid to this house.

"Gentlemen, I thank you for having permitted me to say publicly what has been in my thoughts for sixty years. I thank you for this festival and for your welcome, and I thank the town of Dôle, which never loses sight of any of her children, and which has held me in such affectionate memory."

But the honours paid to his genius, whether of a private or public character, failed to turn him aside from his laborious task. At the beginning of the month of August, 1883, at which time a formidable epidemic of cholera had broken out in Egypt, he sent out a small band of his pupils, Messrs. Roux, Nocard, Strauss and Thuillier, for the purpose of studying the frightful malady and seeking some means of checking its ravages. Thuillier was destined to die during this scientific expedition, stricken down by the scourge in the fullness of youth and hope; he was only twenty-six years of age. Through the pious cares of the Pasteur Institute his medallion has been placed upon one of the walls of the garden, in testimony of his valour and devotion.

The studies pursued by Pasteur and his pupils were at this epoch extended to every malady of microbic origin, but more particularly to hydrophobia, that terror of the country districts, and which the illustrious scientist was determined to vanquish by the combined power of genius and persistence. He was interrupted for a few weeks by the obligation of representing France at the celebration of the tri-centenary of the University of Edinburgh, in company with Messrs. Caro, Gréard, de Lesseps, Guizot and Eugène Guillaume. In London the French delegates found a private parlor car awaiting them, thanks to Mr. Younger, a Scotch brewer, who wished in this manner to thank Pasteur for his studies in relation to beer. It was a recognition of the fine generosity of the French savant, who had enriched commerce and manufactures to the extent of millions, while refusing to retain anything for himself. And that is one of the brightest sides of the glory of France.

Chapter Eight - Hydrophobia

MAD dogs were formerly the terror of the country-side. The mysterious character of the malady, its frightful consequences to those whom it attacked, classed it among those scourges of the fields against which no certain remedy was known. In ancient times Pliny the Elder advised those who had been bitten to eat the liver of the dog who had done the harm, while Gallian prescribed as a remedy the eyes of crabs! During the middle ages, which were haunted by mad dogs, the remedies used were omelettes made of ground oyster shells and cauterisation of the wound with red-hot irons; but most frequently they stifled the unhappy sufferers between two mattresses. In the eighteenth century a Lieutenant of Police named Lenoir founded a prize of twelve hundred pounds, to be awarded by the Royal Society of Medicine to the author of the best paper on the methods of curing hydrophobia. It was won by a certain Dr. Roux, a physician at Dijon, and, among the methods of saving those who had been bitten, he recommended cauterisation with hot irons, and more especially with antimony tri-chloride ("butter of antimony").

In the eighteenth century the problem of hydrophobia, although it had been studied more scientifically, had made but little progress, until Pasteur caused a sensation by discovering its solution. He began his researches in 1880 with the collaboration of Doctors Chamberland, Roux and Thuillier. We cannot follow them through all the details of the long succession of exceedingly delicate experiments that often had to be commenced all over again in order to obtain assured results; but a very simple summary will make it clear that Pasteur's genius was as fruitful as ever, and that his illness had in no wise impaired his qualities as an experimenter.

On the 10th of December, 1880, Pasteur, being informed by Dr. Lannelongue that he had under treatment, at Trousseau a five-year-old child who had been bitten by a mad dog, went to obtain a specimen of his saliva. In the saliva he discovered a microbe, which was not that of hydrophobia, and which, when injected into rabbits, caused their death within two days of a different disease. Nevertheless, the saliva contained the microbes of hydrophobia, but they lost all their virulence within twenty-four hours. Since rabies chiefly affects the nerve centres, Pasteur inoculated rabbits and dogs with the cranial marrow of rabid dogs. The subjects inoculated developed hydrophobia after a greater or less lapse of time, and the experiments became difficult to follow and to control. In order to hasten the period of inoculation, Pasteur conceived the idea of injecting the matter containing the germs directly into the dogs' skulls; but the idea of trepanning, necessitated by the injection, was repugnant to him.

"He could witness, without much distress, a simple operation such as subcutaneous inoculation," writes M. Roux, "although even then, if the animal cried a little, Pasteur would be overcome with pity and make his escape, lavishing on the victim words of consolation and encouragement, which would have seemed comical if they had not been so touching. The thought that a dog's skull would have to be perforated was most unpleasant to him. He was keenly anxious to have the experiment tried, yet he shrank from seeing it undertaken. I did it one day when he was absent. The following day, when I reported to him that the intracranial inoculation offered no difficulties, he fell to pitying the dog:

"'Poor beast! Its brain is no doubt ruptured; it must be paralysed.'

"Without reply, I descended to the basement to get the animal, and brought it back with me to the laboratory. Pasteur was not fond of dogs, but when he saw this one, full of spirits and curiously exploring the premises, he exhibited the keenest satisfaction and began to lavish terms of endearment upon it. He felt an infinite gratitude towards this particular dog for having stood the trepanning so well, and thus having put an end to all his scruples in regard to future trepanning." [1]

The experiment succeeded, and the period of inoculation was reduced to twenty days, and it was demonstrated that the principal seat of the malady was in the nervous centres. To the first results, which were of a theoretic character, Pasteur became ambitious to add others of a practical nature. Was it possible to render dogs immune to hydrophobia after they had been bitten, as he had rendered cattle and sheep immune to anthrax? And could this immunity be extended to man?

The problem was quite complex, for he did not know the microbe of hydrophobia, which had barely been detected by Dr. Roux, in the form of points almost imperceptible under the most powerful microscopes. It was here that the inventive genius of Pasteur displayed itself. Since he could not cultivate these microbes in appropriate liquids and attenuate them according to the method that he had used in the case of anthrax and chicken cholera, he conceived the idea of cultivating them from rabbit to rabbit, and in this way he obtained a fixed maximum of virulence which reduced the period of inoculation to seven days. But how was the virus to be transformed into vaccine? Pasteur observed that the infected marrows, when brought into contact with dry air, lost their virulence in proportion to the length of time they were exposed, becoming almost harmless after fifteen days.

The attenuated virus having been found by a process which, although hardly scientific, was certain, the next facts to ascertain were: First, whether inoculation with this vaccine virus would render dogs resistant to hydrophobia; and, secondly, whether inoculation would prevent the disease from appearing and developing in animals that had been bitten.

The experiments were long and full of difficulties. The laboratory in the Rue d'Ulm no longer sufficed to contain all the subjects. The State placed at Pasteur's disposal more extensive quarters at Villeneuve-l'Etang, near Saint-Cloud. Finally his experiments achieved this double result: Hydrophobia could be communicated to animals by inoculation; and, on the other hand, inoculation with attenuated virus rendered dogs resistant to hydrophobia, and prevented the disease from appearing in those that had been bitten.

Pasteur was sure of the efficacy of his discovery, but he hesitated to apply his method to human beings.

"I have not yet dared to make any attempt upon man," he wrote to the Emperor of Brazil, "in spite of my confidence as to the result, and in spite of the numerous opportunities that have been offered me since my last lecture at the Academy of Sciences. I am too much afraid of a failure, which may compromise my future plans. I want first to collect a multitude of successful cases of the treatment of animals. In this respect matters are going well. I already have numerous examples of dogs rendered immune after having been bitten. I take two dogs, and I cause them to be bitten by another dog that is mad. I vaccinate one of them, and I leave the other without treatment; the latter dies of hydrophobia; the one that was vaccinated is immune.

"But, no matter to what extent I should multiply these examples of the prophylaxis of hydrophobia in dogs, it seems to me that my hand would inevitably tremble when the time came to apply the treatment to a human being.

"Here is where the high and powerful initiative of the Sovereign of a State might intervene most profitably for the greatest good of humanity. If I were king or emperor, or even President of the Republic, this is the way in which I should exercise my right to pardon prisoners condemned to death. I should offer the condemned man, through his lawyer, on the eve of his client's execution, the choice between imminent death and an experiment consisting of preventive inoculation of hydrophobia for the purpose of rendering his constitution immune to that disease. Aside from the risks of these experiments, the life of the condemned man would be spared. In case the experiments should succeed — and, in point of fact, I am sure they would — in order to protect society, which had previously condemned the criminal, he could be kept in custody for the rest of his life.

"Every condemned man would accept. For the only thing which a condemned man fears is death.

'This brings me to the question of cholera, which Your Majesty also had the goodness to discuss with me. Neither Doctors Strauss and Roux nor Dr. Koch have succeeded in infecting animals with cholera. Hence there is a great uncertainty regarding the bacillus which Dr. Koch believes to be the cause of cholera. We ought to be allowed to try to give cholera to criminals condemned to death by making them swallow cultures of these bacilli. As soon as the malady should make its appearance the remedies regarded as most efficacious could immediately be administered.

"I attach so much importance to these measures that, if Your Majesty should share my views, I would gladly set out for Rio Janeiro, despite my age and state of health, in order to devote myself to this sort of study of the prophylaxis of hydrophobia, or the contagion of cholera, and the remedies to be applied to it." (Letter cited by M. Vallery-Radot, in *La Vie de Pasteur*.)

His conscience became so troubled by this weight of responsibility that the famous scientist even thought of inoculating himself, when at last his experiments, repeatedly tried upon animals, gave such unmistakable results that he decided to apply his methods to human beings.

The first inoculation was given to a boy nine years old, an Alsatian, named Joseph Meister, who had been seriously bitten by a mad dog on the 6th of July, 1885. He had fourteen wounds, and was in a lamentable state. The treatment began with the injection of the least virulent vaccine obtained from infected marrow fourteen days old. The child stood it admirably, but Pasteur became anxious, distressed to the point of sleeplessness, when it became necessary to pass on to the virulent vaccines. How would the young patient respond to them? He stood them all without any apparent trouble, and two months from the time that he was first attacked not a sign of hydrophobia had developed. Nor did young Meister subsequently ever show any symptom of it.

Then came another lad, who had played the part of hero, a young shepherd by the name of J. B. Jupille, who successfully underwent the second treatment for hydrophobia. This boy, fifteen years of age, had fought with a mad dog on the lands of Villers-Farlay, in the Jura, in order to save his comrades, five other young shepherds. He had been badly bitten in the struggle, and his case was more serious than that of Meister, because a whole week had passed between the day on which he had received his wounds and that on which he could be inoculated. Like the first patient, he received the hypodermic from Dr. Grancher, with the assistance of Vulpian, on Tuesday, October 29th, 1885; and, after a series of injections of vaccines, he was immune to hydrophobia.

It was at the meeting of the Academy of Sciences, held October 26th, 1885, that Pasteur made his communication on the subject of hydrophobia, preventive vaccination and vaccination after bites, as applied to men. Dr. Vulpian responded and paid homage to the genius of Pasteur:

"The Academy will not be surprised if, as a member of the section of medicine and surgery, I ask the floor in order to express the sentiments of admiration inspired in me by the communication of M. Pasteur. These will be shared, I am convinced, by the medical profession as a whole.

"Hydrophobia, that terrible disease against which all therapeutic efforts have hitherto failed, has at last found its remedy. M. Pasteur, who has had no precursor but himself along this route, has been led through a series of researches, uninterruptedly pursued for years, to create a method of treatment by the aid of which it is possible to prevent, beyond all question, the development of hydrophobia in a man recently bitten by a mad dog. I say, beyond all question, because, after what I have seen in M. Pasteur's laboratory, I cannot myself doubt the permanent success of this treatment, whenever it is applied in its full extent within a few days after the bite has been received.

"It becomes at once necessary to take steps towards the organisation of a public system of treatment for hydrophobia, according to the Pasteur method. Every individual bitten by a mad dog ought to be able to benefit by this great discovery, which puts the seal of glory upon our illustrious colleague, and is destined to redound greatly to the honour of our country."

It was Pasteur's destiny never to triumph through any of his discoveries until after he had overcome desperate resistance. The value of his method was questioned by a large part of the profession, he was ridiculed, and the comic papers published caricatures upon his work.

Pasteur's enemies, who had not even yet disarmed in the presence of his genius, renewed their attacks in connection with a failure which occurred in December, 1885, the death of a young girl, Louise Lepelletier, who had been inoculated thirty-seven days after she was bitten. Nevertheless, all resistance and all perfidy disappeared beneath the immense flood of enthusiasm which had been aroused by Pasteur's discoveries. A public system of vaccination against hydrophobia was installed, and people flocked there from all parts of France and from every other country. Within one year and two months, from October, 1885, to December, 1886, 2,682 persons who had been bitten were treated there, and out of this number only 31 succumbed. The efficacy of the method had been demonstrated.

Pasteur took an interest in the children whom he treated, and lavished caresses and presents on them. He wrote to them, after the course of treatment was over, trying to keep watch of their subsequent lives, and urging upon them the advantages of honesty and industry. The great man, surrounded with the halo of glory, and over-burdened with his labours and his thoughts, found himself paternally drawn towards these little ones — and they were his best source of repose.

[1] *L'Oeuvre Medicate de Pasteur,* by Dr. Roux. Agenda du Chimiste, 1896.

Chapter Nine - The Pasteur Institute

AFTER the close of the war of 1870 Pasteur wrote to Émile Duclaux, expressing his great desire to gather all his pupils into one establishment of which he should be the master, and where they could work together for science and the cure of disease, in accordance with his system and fertile methods. More than twenty years were destined to pass before he saw the realisation of this wish that was so dear to him, and he was not only infirm but almost helpless when he entered the building that was to bear his name.

Thanks to the movement of universal enthusiasm aroused by his cure for hydrophobia, an international subscription was opened, upon the initiative of the Academy of Sciences, for the purpose of founding an establishment for vaccination and for scientific studies, under the title of the Pasteur Institute. Within a few months the modest mites of the poor and the bank notes of the rich and generous formed a sum amounting to 2,586,680 francs (approximately $517,336.00), and the Institute buildings, slowly constructed, were inaugurated by the President of the Republic, Sadi-Carnot, on the 14th of November, 1888. The ceremony took place in the library hall before a gathering including delegations from learned societies, cabinet ministers, members of the Committee of the Institute, presided over by Joseph Bertrand, prominent statesmen and former government officials. Doctor Grancher, treasurer of the Committee, who had been one of the first to recognise the value of the method of vaccinating against hydrophobia, celebrated the discoveries of the illustrious scientist, now so nearly vanquished in life's struggle.

"You know," he said to his eminent hearers, "that M. Pasteur is an innovator, that his creative imagination, controlled by a rigorous observation of facts, has overthrown many errors, and built up in their place an entirely new science. His discoveries relating to ferments, to the generation of infinitely small organisms, and to microbes as the cause of contagious diseases have constituted, in biological chemistry, in the veterinary art and in medicine, not a regular process, but a radical revolution. Now revolutions, even those inspired by scientific demonstrations, leave behind them wherever they pass some victims who do not easily forgive. Consequently M. Pasteur has a number of adversaries scattered throughout the world, not to count those French Athenians who do not like to see the same man always in the right and always fortunate. And, as though his adversaries were not already numerous enough, M. Pasteur made himself others by the implacable rigour of his dialectics and the dogmatic form that he sometimes gives to his thoughts."

To this discourse of Dr. Grancher Pasteur replied in lofty and noble words, in which there was a blending of melancholy and pride and of the deep confidence that he had in the powers of science.

"And on the day when, foreseeing the future possibilities that would be opened up by the discovery of the virus" — so ran the words delivered by his son, for Pasteur himself was too much overcome by suffering and emotion to deliver them in person — "I appealed directly to my country to enable us by means of private subscriptions to build laboratories designed not only for the treatment of hydrophobia, but also for the study of virulent and contagious diseases, that same day France gave to us with lavish hands ...

"And here we see it finished, this grand building of which it may be truly said that there is not a single stone that is not the material sign of a generous thought. All the virtues have paid tribute towards the erection of this abode of toil.

"Alas, it is my most poignant sorrow that I enter it as a man already vanquished by age, no longer surrounded by any of my former masters, nor any of the companions of my struggles, neither Dumas, nor Bouley, nor Paul Bert, nor Vulpian, who, after having been, like you, my dear Grancher, the counsellor of my early efforts, became the most convinced and energetic defender of my method!

"And yet, although I grieve to think they are no longer here, after having taken part so valiantly in controversies which I never provoked, but which I was forced to endure; although they cannot hear me proclaim what I owe to their counsels and support; although I feel their absence as keenly as on the day after their death, I have at least the consolation of the thought that all this work which we defended together is destined not to perish. And this faith in our science is shared by the collaborators and disciples here present.

"Hold fast to the enthusiasm, my dear collaborators, which has been yours since the earliest hour, but make strict accuracy its inseparable companion. Assert nothing that cannot be proved in some simple and decisive fashion.

"Cultivate the critical spirit. Taken by itself, it is neither an awakener of ideas nor an incentive to great deeds. But without it nothing is stable. It always has the last word. This which I ask of you, and which you in turn will ask of the disciples whom you train, is the thing which of all others is most difficult for an inventor.

"To believe that you have discovered an important scientific fact, to feel a feverish desire to proclaim it, and yet to force yourself, for days and weeks, sometimes for years, to combat your own discovery, to do your utmost to disprove your own experiments, and to refrain from announcing what you have discovered until you have exhausted every contrary hypothesis, that indeed is an arduous task.

"But when, after all these efforts, you arrive at certainty, you experience one of the greatest joys that the human soul can know, and the thought that you will contribute to the honour of your country renders this joy even more profound.

"Even if science has no country, the man of science must needs have one, and it is to her that he should give the credit for the influence which his labours may have throughout the world.

"If I may be permitted, Mr. President, to close with a philosophic reflection brought to my mind by your presence in this hall of toil, I would like to say that it seems to me that two contrary laws are today at war: one, a law of blood and death, which, by daily inventing new methods of combat, forces the peoples to be forever ready for the field of battle; and the other, a law of peace and labour and health, which dreams only of delivering mankind from the scourges that beset it.

"The one seeks only violent conquests, the other only the assuagement of human ills. The latter places a single human life above all victories; the former would sacrifice hundreds of thousands of existences to the ambition of one man alone. The law of which we are the instruments seeks, even in the midst of carnage, to stay the bloody havoc wrought by the law of war. The bandaging inspired by our antiseptic methods may preserve thousands of soldiers. Which of these laws will be victorious over the other? God alone knows. But of this we may be assured, that French science will do its utmost, in obedience to the law of humanity, to extend the frontiers of life."

What lofty accents, and how well they sum up the philosophy of the long and laborious effort which Pasteur unfalteringly sustained! He had reached his home, vanquished by life, to use his own expression, but it was peopled by active toilers, his pupils and disciples, who were imbued with his method and would continue to carry on his work, one and all obedient to his temperament and genius as a scientist.

The first buildings, erected on the Rue Dutot, are devoted to the service of the bacteriological Institute. They cover a surface space of eleven thousand square metres, and consist of two vast two-story pavillions, parallel to the street, and connected by a third midway between them.

They contain, besides the laboratories, the study halls, and a library where scientific works may be consulted, and which also contains busts of Pasteur, of Don Pedro, of Alexander III, of Mme. Furtado-Heine, of Mme. Boucicaut, of M. A. de Rothschild and of the Count de Laubespin, all benefactors of the Institute. It is also adorned by two paintings, the one representing Émile Duclaux, the other Professor Metchnikoff. Work in this fine and spacious chamber is facilitated by the cordial welcome of its librarian, M. Roussel. An apartment has been reserved for Pasteur; it is at present occupied by Dr. Roux, director of the institute.

All the working rooms, whatever their dimensions, are finished according to the same model, without colours, and with varnished walls, with the result that there is always the most absolute cleanliness.

The department for the treatment of hydrophobia is installed on the ground floor; it includes a waiting room, an examination room, an inoculation room, besides a laboratory, in which are preserved the marrows of infected rabbits, which are used for the preparation of vaccines. In the left wing are situated a lecture room, a laboratory for the preparation of culture mediums and a dissecting room. The first floor is given over to the course in the technical study of microbes, and the second floor is used for the researches of young scientists who have been admitted for the purpose of carrying on their personal studies.

The active work of the Bacteriological Institute is divided into four main branches: the department of vaccines, the department of hydrophobia, the department of technical microbiology, and the department of Metchnikoff.

After the erection of the Bacteriological Institute, the Serotherapic Institute was founded, as a result of the discovery, by Dr. Roux, of the vaccine for croup, and, next, the Institute of Biological Chemistry.

Page from Pasteur's Note-Book, while Professor of Chemistry (Preserved at the _École Normale_)

69

The Pasteur Institute, as a collective whole, which had for its first director the illustrious scientist, Émile Duclaux, forms a vast organism, in which the most precious discoveries are evolved. It is frequented by large numbers of students, both native and foreign. It has thrown forth branches throughout the world, and there is today no country that does not possess a Pasteur Institute. We find them in Russia, Turkey, Italy, Brazil, the Argentine Republic, the French colonies, Tunis, Indo-China, Morocco, Cambodia, etc. Every year a new building rises in some corner of the earth where there is some special malady to conquer, and whither a remedy may be brought. Commissions set forth from the Institute in the Rue Dutot to go and study on the spot these great epidemics, the modern scourges which must be conquered.

The Pasteur Institute, today directed by Dr. Roux, is an incomparable working laboratory, in which the most precious discoveries are being evolved, and it is also an admirable instrument for the promulgation of France's contributions to science.

Chapter Ten - The Supreme Homage

PASTEUR was seventy years of age. From his earliest years of study he had consecrated his life to science, and unwaveringly, with tireless energy, that neither envious attacks nor bodily illness could break down, he had pursued, through a chain of strong and harmonious logic, the revolution which his genius had introduced into science and medicine. Now, in spite of the last selfish resistance of those who were not willing to surrender to the evidence of the truth, his name had become famous throughout the world, his methods were introduced into numberless laboratories, his discoveries were everywhere being applied with success. Pasteur, bowed with suffering and with years, almost incapacitated to do further work, was surrounded by universal admiration and by the personal affection of that group of scientists who, within his Institute, were pursuing their personal researches along the path that he had traced.

It was at this epoch that various committees were formed, both in France and abroad, for the purpose of celebrating the seventieth anniversary of his birth. The movement emanated from Denmark, Sweden and Norway, while at Paris the Academy of Sciences was deeply stirred, on the 7th of November, 1892, by a letter from its section of medicine and surgery, asking that homage should be paid to the illustrious scientist.

"Monsieur the President: Monsieur Pasteur will be seventy years of age on the 27th of next December.

"The section of medicine and surgery feels that it ought to take the initiative in celebrating this glorious anniversary. Yet, while medicine and surgery both owe M. Pasteur a boundless admiration and gratitude, we know that the Institute as a whole is united in this same sentiment.

"Accordingly we propose to invite our colleagues in the Institute, as well as all others who have benefitted from the labours and discoveries of M. Pasteur, either in the domain of scientific research, or in the practice of their art, to contribute to a subscription raised for the purpose of offering our illustrious compatriot a souvenir and a homage on the occasion of this jubilee.

"To this end the section of medicine and surgery has constituted itself a subscription committee. M. Duclaux has kindly consented to co-operate with us, and Professor Grancher has undertaken the duties of secretary of the committee.

"We beg that our colleagues will send their offerings to the office of the secretary of the Institute.

"The Members of the Committee:

"Marey, Charcot, Brown-Sequard, Grancher, Bouchard, Verneuil, Guyon, Duclaux."

The Academy of Sciences hastened to comply with the desire of its section of medicine, and at the following meeting Pasteur expressed his thanks to his colleagues.

"I was not present," he said, "at the opening of the last meeting, when the President read the letter from the section of medicine and surgery.

"Someone was kind enough to detain me outside. It was well he did so. I should have been too deeply moved to return adequate thanks to my colleagues for the excessive honour they are preparing for me. Even today I am unable to express all the emotion and gratitude that I feel."

Roty, a member of the Institute, was chosen to execute the medal which was to be presented to him, and Messrs. Bouchard and Guyon undertook to arrange the details of the *Jubilee*.

It took place on December 27th, 1892, in the presence of the President of the Republic, Sadi-Carnot, in the great amphitheatre of the new Sorbonne.

Seated on the platform were to be seen, to the right of the President's chair, Messrs. d'Abbadie. President of the Academy of Sciences; Le Royer, President of the Senate; Ribot, President of the Council of Ministers; the Ambassadors from Russia, England, Austria-Hungary, Belgium, Portugal, the Netherlands, Sweden and Norway, Denmark and Bavaria; on the left, Messrs. Joseph Bertrand, permanent Secretary of the Academy of Sciences; Charles Floquet, President of the Chamber; Charles Dupuy, Minister of Public Instruction, and all the other Ministers. Behind these official personages were the delegations from the Institute, the Academy of Medicine, and foreign scientific societies; M. Greard, Vice-Rector of the Academy of Paris; M. Perrot, Director of the École Normale; the deans of the faculties, the presidents of the Court of Cassation, of the Council of State and of the Court of Appeals.

The auditorium was occupied by delegations from the schools and faculties, the General Association of Students, the hospital staffs, the École Normale Supérieure, the Polytechnique, the Faculty of Medicine, the Faculty of Sciences, and the School of Pharmacy.

It was a chosen assemblage, wrought to the highest pitch of enthusiasm, and comprising representatives of all that was best in art and science and intellectual thought. At half-past ten Louis Pasteur made his entry, leaning on the arm of the President of the Republic, while the band of the Republican Guard saluted him with a triumphal march, and the entire assemblage arose to its feet and acclaimed him with rounds of applause. Pasteur seated himself before a little table on the platform, in order to receive the addresses of the delegates, and the President of the Academy of Sciences, M. d'Abbadie, opened the meeting and gave the floor to M. Charles Dupuy, Minister of Public Instruction. After summing up the works of Pasteur, and extending a greeting to the foreign delegates, M. Dupuy concluded by pointing out the significance of the Jubilee:

"But what characterises this ceremony beyond all else, what gives your Jubilee its distinctive mark," he said, "is that our homage is extended less to the past than to the future; science, on behalf of which the whole universe is in your debt, has received from you a sure method and a definite principle; but, as you yourself have said, the era of its application has only just commenced.

'The Pasteur Institute, built and endowed through the gratitude and admiration of peoples and of governments, for the purpose of serving both as a centre of high scientific culture and as a source of relief for the ills of the human race, will realise your hopes.

"May you long continue, dear and illustrious master, to preside over the destinies of this young and glorious edifice, and animate with your inspiring ardour the phalanx of disciples who will surely fulfil the promises of the Pasteur doctrine. May France possess you for long years yet to come, and distinguish you before the world as the worthy object of her love, her gratitude and her pride."

After M. d'Abbadie had presented Pasteur with the great golden medal engraved by Roty, addresses were made by Messrs. Bertrand and Daubree, and then by the famous English surgeon. Lister, in the name of the Royal Society of London.

"Monsieur Pasteur," he said, "the great honour has been accorded me of bringing you the homage of the sciences of medicine and surgery.

"As a matter of fact, there is no one living in the entire world to whom the medical sciences owe so much as they do to you. Your researches in regard to fermentations have shed a powerful light that has illumined the fatal darkness of surgery and changed the treatment of wounds from a matter of empiricism, uncertain and too often disastrous, to a scientific art of assured beneficence.

"Thanks to you, surgery has undergone a complete revolution which has robbed it of its terrors and extended its efiicacious powers almost without limit.

"Medicine is indebted, no less than surgery, to your profound and philosophic studies. You have lifted the veil which for centuries had overhung infectious diseases. You have discovered and demonstrated their microbic nature; thanks to your initiative, and in many cases to your special and personal labours, there are already a number of these pernicious disorders of the causes of which we have a complete knowledge.

"*Felix qui potuit rerum cognoscere causas.*

'This knowledge has already perfected in a surprising fashion the diagnosis of these scourges of the human race, and has pointed out the path which must be followed in their prophylactic and curative treatment. On this path your fine discoveries of the attenuation and reinforcement of viruses and preventive inoculations serve and will always continue to serve as guiding stars.

"As a brilliant illustration, I may refer to your services in regard to hydrophobia. Their originality is so striking, both in respect to pathology and to therapeutics, that in the beginning many physicians were mistrustful of you.

"'Is it possible,' they said to me, 'that a man who is neither a physician nor a biologist can instruct us after this fashion regarding a disease over which the finest brains in the medical profession have laboured in vain?'

"*Quis novus hic nostris successit sedibus hospes?*

"For my part, I knew only too well the brilliance of your genius, the scrupulous care of your inductions, and your absolute honesty, to share such opinions for a moment. My confidence has been amply justified by the results, because, with the insignificant exception of a few ignorant persons, the whole world now recognises the greatness of your victory over this terrible malady. You have furnished a method of diagnosis which puts an end, beyond question, to the torturing uncertainty which formerly haunted anyone who had been bitten by a dog which, although healthy, was suspected of being mad. This alone would have sufficed to assure you the eternal gratitude of humanity.

"But through your marvellous system of inoculations against hydrophobia you have succeeded in following up the poison after its entry into the system and have vanquished it.

"Monsieur Pasteur, infectious diseases constitute, as you know, the great majority of maladies that afflict the human race. You can therefore well understand that the sciences of medicine and surgery are eager, upon this solemn occasion, to offer you the profound homage of their admiration and gratitude."

At the close of this address the two great scientists exchanged affectionate greetings in the midst of tumultuous enthusiasm. Further addresses were delivered by M. Bergeron, permanent secretary of the Academy of Medicine, and by M. Sauton, President of the Municipal Council of Paris. The delegations then filed past the little table behind which Pasteur was seated, and laid their addresses on it.

England was represented not only by Lister, but by Burdon-Sanderson, Grath, MoUoy, Pavy, Percival Wright, Roscoe, Ray Lancaster, Ruffer, Sydney Martin, Woodhead, Plimmer; Germany by Haskovec and Schottelius; Belgium by Berlier, Van Beneden, Casimir, Depaire, Errera, Laurent, Parmentier, Pechère, Rousseau, Rufferath, de Wilde; Denmark by Jacobsen, Salomonsen, Studgaard, Wanscher; Spain by Chiron and Gener; Holland by Engelmann, Pekelharing, Sponck, Stokvis, Van Overbecle de Meyer; Italy by Campana and Perroncito; Russia by Metchnikoff and Winogradsky; Poland by Benni, Bujwid and Galezowski; Sweden and Norway by Hjartdahl, Malm, Lindstrom, Nordenson, Selander; Switzerland by Cerenville, d'Espine, Ladame, Soret, Tarel, Sulzer. The leading scientific societies also had their delegates; the University of Athens was represented by M. Panas, and the Berlin Society of Medicine and Faculty of Medicine by M. Bouchard. There were still other delegations, from the Society of Medicine at Berne, the Belgian Society of Microscopy, and the Society of Students of the Civil Hospitals of Brussels, from the Academic College of Bucharest and the University of Christiania, from the Association of Hygiene at Cologne, from the Academy of Copenhagen, etc.

The French delegations were called forward in their turn, and those from Dôle and Arbois attracted special attention because, in the midst of this glorious ceremony, they called to mind the humble origin of Pasteur; the mayor of Dôle offered him in the name of its citizens an album containing reproductions of his birth certificate and of the little house in which he was born. This was an intimate note, tender and touching.

Pasteur's reply to these discourses celebrating his glory had to be read by his son; it is a page of grave eloquence, and forms as it were his moral and scientific testament. Here is the complete text, which deserves to be preserved as one of the most beautiful monuments of French thought.

"Monsieur the President of the Republic: Your presence transforms everything; an intimate festival becomes a great festival, and the simple anniversary of the birth of a scientist will remain, thanks to you, a date in the history of French science.

"Monsieur the Minister:

"Gentlemen: In the midst of all this brilliance my first thought reverts regretfully to all those men of science who spent their lives in vain endeavours. In the past they had to struggle against prejudices which stifled their ideas. These prejudices conquered, they still encountered other obstacles and difficulties of all sorts.

"It was only a few years ago, before the public authorities and the municipal council had begun to provide magnificent abodes for science, that a man whom I greatly loved and admired, Claude Bernard, possessed as his sole laboratory a low and humid cellar, only a few steps from here. Perhaps it was in that cellar that he contracted the disease which caused his death. Upon learning of the reception you were preparing for me tonight, his was the first image that rose before my mind. I salute the memory of that great man.

"Gentlemen, though an ingenious and delicate thought, it would seem as though you had wished to cause a vision of my entire life to pass before my eyes. One of my compatriots from the Jura, the mayor of the city of Dôle, has brought me a photograph of the very humble home in which my father and mother lived their hard and needy life.

"The presence of all these students from the École Normale reminds me of the intoxication of my first scientific enthusiasms.

"The representatives of the Faculty of Lille evoke the memory of my first studies in crystalography and fermentations, which opened to me an entire new world. What boundless hopes took possession of me when I first grasped the fact that there were laws behind all those obscure phenomena!

"You, my dear colleagues, have yourselves been witnesses of the series of deductions that permitted me, as a disciple of the experimental method, to arrive at physiological studies. If at times I have troubled the calm of our Academies with somewhat heated discussions, it was because I was passionately defending the truth.

"You, lastly, delegates from foreign nations, who have come from so far to give proof of your sympathy towards France, you bring me the most profound joy that can be felt by a man who believes invincibly that science and peace will triumph over ignorance and war; that the various peoples will come to an agreement not to destroy, but to build up; and that the future will belong to those who have done the most for suffering humanity. I appeal to you, by dear Lister, and to you all, illustrious representatives of science and medicine and surgery.

"Young men, young men, put your confidence in these sure and powerful methods, from which we have as yet learned only the first secrets. And I say to all of you, whatever your career may be, guard yourselves from the taint of destructive and sterile scepticism, refuse to be discouraged by the sadness of certain hours which pass over a nation. Live in the serene peace of laboratories and libraries. Say to yourselves at first: What have I done towards my own education? And then, in proportion as you advance: What have I done for my country? Do so up to the moment when, perhaps, you may have the immense happiness of thinking that you have contributed in some measure to the progress and well-being of humanity. But, whether life favours your efforts to a greater or a less extent, one must have earned the right to say when the great goal draws near: 'I have done what I could.'

"Gentlemen, I wish to express my profound emotion and my deepest gratitude. Just as the great artist, Roty, on the reverse side of this medal, has hidden under roses the date of heavy years that weigh upon my life, so you, my dear colleagues, have wished to give to my old age a spectacle to gladden it immensely, the spectacle of all this eager and affectionate youth."

The ceremony, notwithstanding that it was official, ended in an outburst of enthusiasm that gave it a high human significance.

Louis Pasteur had fulfilled his task. The robust toiler, genius and dogged will combined, could now rest among his disciples, who continued the struggle in his place and according to his methods on behalf of science and against disease, in order to "extend the frontiers of life."

Chapter Eleven - The Last Days of a Great Man

EVER since his first attacks of paralysis Pasteur had retained a certain heaviness in his movements, and, while his brain was intact, experiments demanding a supreme manual dexterity had become difficult for him. He was forced regretfully to abandon his labours, still unsatisfied with what he had achieved, and with his imagination still active and dreaming of discoveries that still evaded him. Pasteur continued to follow the experiments of his disciples, which were born of his methods, but what he wanted was the power to push onward by himself to the extreme limits of the new path which his genius had laid open. However, he accepted his destiny without bitterness. He was able to share the delight of Dr. Roux when the latter's labours resulted in the discovery of a vaccine for diphtheria, which had previously decimated the lives of children. Then croup was vanquished, just as rabies and anthrax had been before it; thousands of existences, and those of the most precious sort, for the future of the race slumbered in them, had thus been saved. Dr. Yersin, for his part, discovered the microbe of the plague; while the whole band of workers, who had come to be known as "Pasteurians," each following his individual aptitudes and tastes, rivalled one another in zealous service of science and humanity.

It was at this period of researches and discoveries, based on his doctrines and his processes as an experimenter, that Louis Pasteur was attacked by the malady from which he was destined to die. On the 1st of November, 1894, he had an attack of uremia, and there followed a long, slow agony, lasting for months, with alternations of hope and despair. Pasteur endured it with Christian resignation, for science in his case had in no way destroyed faith, and throughout his life he had remained a practical Catholic. His pupils took turns in watching beside him, thus showing that he had not only been able to arouse their scientific enthusiasm, but had also attached them to him by his kindliness and bigness of heart.

"At the end of December," writes M. Vallery-Radot, "we began to have hope. On the 1st of January, after receiving all of his collaborators down to the youngest of the laboratory attendants, Pasteur saw one of his colleagues of the Académie Française enter the room.

"It was Alexandre Dumas. He had a bouquet of roses with him, and was accompanied by one of his daughters.

"'I wanted to begin the year well,' he said; 'I bring you all my best wishes.'"

Ever since they first met, twelve years before, on a certain Thursday at the Académie Française, Alexandre Dumas and Pasteur had felt themselves mutually drawn towards each other. Pasteur, charmed at first by the swift deductions of this brilliant mind, had been surprised, touched, deeply moved by the courtesies and delicate attentions that were prompted by a heart which opened to friendship all the more widely because it opened only in deep earnest. Dumas, who had a wide experience of men, loved and admired Pasteur as a genius without pride and full of kindliness. On this New Year's afternoon he fell to chatting with a cordiality that contained something of the unquenchable gaiety of his father. In this little chamber adjoining the laboratory, how remote he was from all the worlds that he had studied, the worlds inhabited by the class of beings he had studied, "microbes in human form," as he called them, creatures that were either dangerous, ridiculous or vile! Occasionally, however, he had shown upon the stage man as he might be, and as he ought to be, a Montaiglin, a Claude, "poor, well-meaning man, out of place in our times." For back of this dramatic author was a man eager to exert a moral influence, back of the realist a symbolist, back of the satirist a mystic. After having hungered for glory he placed higher than all else the desire to be useful. And the glance of his blue eyes, ordinarily cold and keen, seeming to penetrate one's most secret thoughts, this glance, always on guard, always ironic, took on an expression of affectionate veneration for him whom he called "our dear and great Pasteur." It is only those who are accustomed to tend the sick can know how much pleasure certain visits give them. That of Alexandre Dumas Pasteur compared to a ray of sunshine. (*Vie de Pasteur.*)

The illustrious old man still had a few more happy hours before him; but, although he was removed to Villeneuve-l'Étang, the change to the country brought no improvement to his condition, which had now become hopeless.

Pasteur resigned himself to die, and nevertheless he took great care to hide his sufferings, in order to spare the feelings of his family and his disciples. He was not, however, always master of his own emotions. Happening, one evening, to be alone with his grandchildren, the son and daughter of M. and Mme. Vallery-Radot, he took them in his arms and kissed them lingeringly, while heavy tears rolled slowly down the length of his pain-racked face. When the startled children questioned him, the great man answered sorrowfully:

"I am weeping, my children, because I am so soon to leave you."

It was during the afternoon of Wednesday, September 27, that the Cure of Garches was summoned to the side of Pasteur, whose end was felt to be very near. He received extreme unction, after having made confession to R. P. Boulanger, of the Dominican order. He died the following morning at twenty minutes to five after a brief agony.

It was a universal calamity. Telegrams poured into the Institute, and there is one of them which must be cited in full, and which came from the establishment in Berlin directed by Dr. Koch, who had so often had occasion to combat him:

PASTEUR'S TOMB - It is in the Rue Dutot, beneath the principal entrance to the Pasteur Institute, in a crypt lined with marble, that one of the most glorious representatives of universal science has found his last resting place.

"Profoundly moved by the loss which is universally felt, and which the Pasteur Institute has just sustained in the person of its gifted founder, the Berlin Institute of Infectious Diseases expresses its heartfelt participation in the general sorrow."

The Government decided that the obsequies of Louis Pasteur should be national and that the State should bear the expense. They were conducted with full official pomp and before an immense public gathering, on October 5th, 1895. The religious ceremony, presided over by Monseigneur Richard, was conducted at Notre-Dame, in the presence of the President of the Republic, Felix Faure, the Grand Duke Constantine of Russia, and Prince Nicholas of Greece. At its conclusion M. Poincare delivered an admirable address in the name of the Government beside the bier, where it rested before the threshold of Notre Dame.

"Science," he said, "will never weary. Messieurs, of admiring in the genius of Pasteur the combined force of a creative imagination and the most rigorous experimental method.

"He had sudden inspirations, which bore him on towards unexpected discoveries; he had instincts of divination which pushed him forward along unexplored paths; he had swift, headlong rushes of thought that overleaped and anticipated the establishment of the truth, prepared the way for it, made its attainment more rapid and more sure. But when a scientific problem had taken shape before him, in one of those general flashes of illumination, he never considered it as solved until he had questioned all nature, until he had classified or eliminated all of the facts, until he had forced them, each and every one, to give him an answer.

"He was careful to guard against any philosophical prejudice that might hamper the sincerity of his observations. The experimental method, he declared in his address at the time of his reception at the Academie, should be detached from all metaphysical speculation, and, while claiming for his conscience the right to assert loudly its spiritual and religious convictions, he claimed no less energetically all the prerogatives of liberty on behalf of science. And it was really the unrestrained curiosity of his searching mind, spurred on by his inventive powers, and seconded by his scrupulous research for objective truths, that guided him through the long and brilliant evolution of his scientific labours..."

"Happy is he," said Pasteur; "happy is he who carries within him his own ideal, and lives in obedience to it." Throughout his life Pasteur himself lived in obedience to the highest and purest of ideals, in science and virtue and charity. All his thoughts and all his actions were illumined by the reflected rays of that inner flam^; he owed his greatness to his sensibilities; and posterity will assign him a place in the radiant line of apostles of goodness and of truth.

The body of Louis Pasteur was interred in the Institute, and there he lies, in the cold and austere crypt, while men of learning, inspired by his genius, continue and carry towards completion his work that was so prolific for the advance of science and for the good of humanity.

The illustrious savant was one of the greatest of modern heroes, and we may well conclude with the words of Émile Duclaux:

"There is no other example in science of a savant who has been privileged to see the domain which he discovered expand and bear fruit to such an extent. Perhaps Lavoisier, whose name comes naturally to mind in speaking of Pasteur, might have had the joy of seeing himself equally great, if he had been able to keep on to the end of his career. The only exact comparison is that of a Napoleon dying triumphant in the midst of Europe permanently conquered and pacified. Even that vision, magnificent as it is, is incomplete: Pasteur conquered the world, yet his glory did not cost a single tear."

END

Brief Index of the Principal Names Cited

BASTIAN, Henry Charlton, English physician, born at Truro, Cornwall, April 26, 1837. Author of numerous works, among others, *The Modes of Origin of Lowest Organisms; The Beginnings of Life; Clinical Lectures on the Common Forms of Paralysis from Brain Disease.*

BERT, Paul, French physiologist and statesman, born at Auxerre in 1833, died at Hanoi in 1886.

BIOT, Jean Baptiste, astronomer, mathematician, physicist, and chemist, born at Paris in 1774, died at Paris in 1862. He participated in efforts undertaken in Spain to measure the meridian, and has left important writings on polarisation, stellar astronomy, etc.

BUFFON, Georges Louis Leclerc, Comte de, naturalist and one of the greatest of French writers, born at Montbard, Cote-d'Or, in 1707, died at Paris in 1788. Author of a Natural History and a *Treatise on the Epochs of Nature.* Member of the Académie Française.

DAGUERRE, Louise Jacques Mende, inventor of the diorama and one of the inventors of photography, born at Cormeilles-en-Parisis (Seineet-Oise) in 1789, died at Bry-sur-Marne in 1851.

DAVAINE, Casimir Joseph, French physician, born at Saint-Amand-les-Eaux in 1812, died at Garches in 1882, author of remarkable treatises on experimental physiology. His discovery, in 1850, of the bacteria of anthrax makes him the true precursor of Pasteur.

DELAFOSSE, Gabriel, French mineralogist, born at Saint-Quentin in 1796, died at Paris in 1878. He occupied the chair of mineralogy in the Paris Faculty of Sciences and in the École Normale, and in 1857 was elected member of the Academy of Sciences. Delafosse devoted himself in a very special way to the study of crystalography.

DUMAS, Jean Baptiste, chemist, born at Alais (Gard) in 1800, died at Cannes in 1884. He was elected member of the Academy of Sciences in 1832, then professor in the Faculty of Sciences of Paris, the Faculty of Medicine and the College de France. He was the founder of the Normal School of Arts and Sciences. Dumas was a member of the Institute, permanent secretary of the Academy of Sciences, and member of the Académie Française (1875). He was the author of a great Treatise on Chemistry applied to the Arts.

FRÉMY, Edmond, French chemist, born at Versailles in 1814, died at Paris in 1894. Author of remarkable researches relating to the fatty acids.

GUÉRIN, Jules Rene, French surgeon, born at Boussu, Belgium, in 1801, died at Hyeres in 1886.

HAÜY, Abbé René Just, French mineralogist, born at Saint-Just, Oise, in 1743, died at Paris in 1822. He founded the science of crystalography.

HELMHOLTZ, Hermann von, German physiologist and physicist, born at Potsdam in 1821, died at Charlottenburg in 1894. Author of remarkable works on optics, electricity and acoustics.

HERSCHEL, Sir William, celebrated astronomer, born in Hanover in 1738, died at Slough, near Windsor, in 1822. He was the founder of the science of stellar astronomy.

JOLY, Nicolas, French zoologist, born at Toul July 11th, 1812. Author of numerous works, including *Researches in Regard to Silk Worms and Their Diseases,* 1858; *Researches into the Origin, Germination and Fructification of Brewer's Yeast.*

KOCH, Robert, German physician and microbiologist, born at Klausthal, Hanover, in 1843. He has published remarkable researches in tuberculosis, the bacilli of which he discovered and succeeded in cultivating.

LAVOISIER, Antoine Laurent, famous French chemist, born at Paris in 1743, died in Paris in 1794. One of the founders of modern chemistry, on the basis of a previously unknown law, that of the conservation of matter: "Nothing is lost, nothing is created."

LIEBIG, Justus, Baron von, German chemist, born at Darmstadt in 1803, died at Munich in 1873. He was one of the first to apply chemical analysis to the phenomena of organic life.

LITTRÉ, Maximilien Paul Émile, French philologist and philosopher of the positivist school, born at Paris in 1801, died at Paris in 1881. His principal work is his *Dictionary of the French Language.* He was a member of the Academic Frangaise.

MITSCHERLICH, Eilhard, German chemist, born at Neuende in 1794, died at Schoeneberg in 1863. He was the discoverer of the law of isomorphism.

NEEDHAM, John Tuberville, English physicist, born at London in 1713, died at Brussels in 1781.

NIEPCE, Joseph Nicephore, French chemist, born at Chalon-sur-Saone in 1765, died in. the same town in 1833. With Daguerre, he was one of the inventors of photography.

NISARD, Jean Marie Napoléon Désiré, French man of letters, born at Châtillon-sur-Seine in 1806, died at San Remo in 1883. He was director of the École Normale Superieure and member of the Académie Française.

PARACELSUS (his real name . being Philippus Aureolus Theophrastus Bombast von Hohenheim), a celebrated Swiss physician and alchemist, born at Einsiedeln, in the canton of Schwyz, December 11th, 1493, died at Salzburg September 24th, 1541. He may be regarded as the founder of the modern doctrine of *specifics.*

POUCHET, Felix Archimède, French naturalist, born at Rouen in 1800, died in that same city in 1872. He was celebrated for his controversies with Pasteur on the subject of spontaneous generation.

QUATREFAGES, Jean Louis Armand de Bréau de, French naturalist and anthropologist, born at Berthezène, Gard, in 1810, died at Paris in 1892. He defended the theory of the unity of the origin of man.

REGNAULT, Henri Victor, French physicist and chemist, born at Aix-la-Chapelle July 11th, 1810, died at Paris January 19th, 1878.

ROUX, Pierre Paul Émile, French physician, born at Confolens, Charente, December 17th, 1853. Member of the Academy of Medicine arid the Academy of Sciences. Director of the Pasteur Institute.

SCHULTZE, Max Johann Sigismond, German anatomist, born at Freiburg-im-Breisgau March 15th, 1825, died at Bonn January 16th, 1874. He was appointed professor at Bonn in 1859, and there founded an important anatomical institute.

SPALLANZANI, Lazaro, Italian naturalist, born at Scandiano in 1729, died at Pavia in 1799. He was the author of important works upon the circulation of the blood, the digestion, reproduction, and microscopic animals.

THÉNARD, Louis Jacques, Baron, learned French chemist, collaborator of Gay-Lussac, born at La Louptiere, Aube, in 1777, died at Paris in 1857. He was the discoverer of hydrogen peroxide, boron, etc. Pasteur delivered a discourse at the unveiling of his monument.

TROUSSEAU, Armand, French physician, born at Tours in 1801, died at Paris in 1867. He was author of a *Treatise on Therapeutics,* which for a long time remained a classic.

TYNDALL, John, English physicist, born at Leighlin Bridge, Ireland, in 1820, died at Hind Head in 1893. Author of remarkable works upon heat and electricity.

VAN TIEGHEM, Philippe Edguard Léon, French botanist, member of the Institute, born at Bailleul, Nord, April 19th, 1839, was a student at the École Normale from 1858 to 1861, and later became a lecturer in the same school. Member of the Academy of Sciences.

VICAT, Louis Joseph, French engineer, born at Nevers, March 31st, 1786, died at Grenoble April 10th, 1861. Author of memorable works on hydraulic limes and cements.

Principal Publications, Articles, Monographs, etc., of Louis Pasteur

1848 Notes on the Crystallization of Sulphur.
Researches into the different Modes of grouping in Sulphate of Potash.
Researches in Dimorphism.
Memorandum on the Relation which may exist between crystalline Form and chemical Composition and on the Cause of rotary Polarization.
Researches into the Relations which may exist between crystalline Form, chemical Composition and the Direction of the rotary Power.

Researches into the Relations which may exist between crystalline Form, chemical Composition and the Direction of rotary Polarization (2d Memorandum).

1849 Researches into the specific Properties of the two Acids which compose racemic Acid.

1850 New Researches into the Relations which may exist between crystalline Form, chemical Composition and the Phenomenon of rotary Polarization.

New Researches into the Relations which may exist between crystalline Form, chemical Composition and molecular rotary Power.

1851 Memorandum upon aspartic and malic Acid.

Regarding a Memorandum relative to aspartic and malic Acid.

1852 Observations upon artificial Populin and Salicin.

New Researches into the Relations which may exist between crystalline Form, chemical Composition and the molecular rotary Phenomenon.

1853 New Facts relating to the History of racemic Acid (M. Kestner's Letter to M. Biot). Notes on the Origin of racemic Acid.

Notes on Quinidine.

New Researches into the Relations which may exist between crystalline Form, chemical Composition and the molecular rotary Phenomenon.

Note upon Quinidine.

Transformation of tartaric Acid into racemic Acid.

Researches into the Alcaloids of the Cinchonas.

Transformation of the tartaric Acids into racemic Acid. Discovery of inactive tartaric Acid. New Method of separating racemic Acid into right and left tartaric Acid.

1854 Regarding Dimorphism.

1855 Memorandum upon amylic Alcohol.

1856 Note upon Sugar and Milk.

Isomorphism between isomeric Bodies, some active and others inactive, in relation to polarized Light.

Studies regarding the Methods of Growth of Crystals and the Causes of their Secondary Forms.

1857 Memorandum upon so-called lactic Fermentation.

Memorandum upon alcoholic Fermentation.

1858 Upon alcoholic Fermentation.

Memorandum upon the Fermentation of tartaric Acid.

Constant Production of Glycerine in alcoholic Fermentation.

New Researches into alcoholic Fermentation.

New Facts concerning the History of alcoholic Fermentation.

1859 New Facts contributing to the History of lactic Yeast.

New Facts concerning alcoholic Fermentation.

New Facts relating to alcoholic Fermentation, Cellulose and the fatty Matters in Yeast formed at the expense of Sugar.

Note upon the Remarks Presented by M. Berthelot at the last Session of the Academy.

Memorandum upon alcoholic Fermentation.

1860 Extract from the Report upon the Competition for the Prize in experimental Physiology for the year 1859. *Monthyon Foundation.*

Experiments relating to so-called spontaneous Generation.

On the Origin of Ferments. New Experiments relating to so-called spontaneous Generation.

Note on so-called alcoholic Fermentation.

Note relating to the *Penicilium Glaucum* and to the molecular Dissymmetry of natural organic Products.

New Experiments relating to so-called spontaneous Generation.

Researches into the Mode of Nutrition of the *Mucedineae.*

1861 Continuation of a previous Communication relating to so-called spontaneous Generation.

The Influence of Temperature upon the Fertility of Spores of the *Mucedineae.*

Infusorial Animalcula living without free oxygen Gas and producing Fermentations.

Memorandum upon organic Corpuscles which exist in the Atmosphere. Examination of the Doctrine of spontaneous Generation.

New Experiments and Views regarding the nature of Fermentations.

Rectification of a Passage in a Note presented to the Academy by Messrs. Joly and Musset.

1862 Studies of the Mycoderms. The Rôle played by these Plants in acetic Fermentation.

New industrial Process for the Manufacture of Vinegar.

1863 New Example of Fermentation determined by infusorial Animalcula which can live without free Oxygen Gas and apart from any Contact with atmospheric Air.

Examination of the Rôle attributed to atmospheric Oxygen Gas in the Destruction of animal and vegetable Matter after Death.

Note on the Presence of acetic Acid among the Products of alcoholic Fermentation.

Remarks on the Subject of the note communicated by M. Van Thiéghem at the last Session of the Academy.

Note relative to a Communication from M. Béchamp inserted in the Secretary's Report of the last Session.

Researches in Regard to Putrefaction.

Note. In Response to critical Observations presented to the Academy by Messrs. Pouchet, Joly and Musset, at the Session on the 21st of last September.

Remarks on the Occasion of a new Note from Messrs. Joly and Musset relative to the same Question.

Studies on Wines. First Part: the Influence of atmospheric Oxygen in Vinification.

Note relative to the Claims of Priority raised by M. Béchamp, in Regard to my Works on Fermentations and so-called spontaneous Generation.

1864 Notes on spontaneous Generation.

Studies of Wines. Second Part: spontaneous

Alterations or Maladies of Wines, especially in the Jura.

Note in Response to the Remarks of M. Pouchet relative to spontaneous Generation.

Remarks on the Occasion of a Request by

Messrs. Pouchet, Joly and Musset to await the Return of the warm Season before repeating their Experiments in Heterogenesis.

Communication from M. Pasteur presenting the first Number of the *Annales Scientifiques de l'Ecole Normale,* which was published under his Direction.

Remarks on the Occasion of a Memorandum by Messrs. Bussy and Buignet on the Changes of Temperature produced by the Mixture of Liquids produced by separate Cultures.

1865 Report upon Experiments relating to spontaneous Generation.

Practical Process for preserving and improving Wines.

Note on the Deposits that are formed in Wines.

New Observations on the Subject of the preservation of Wines.

Note on the Occasion of a Communication from Messrs. Leplat and Jaillard concerning the Disease of splenic Apoplexy (*sang de rate*).

Observations on the Diseases of Silk-worms.

Note accompanying the Presentation of a Pamphlet on the Preservation of Wines.

Notes on the Employment of Heat as a means of preserving Wines.

1866 New Studies on the Disease of Silk-worms.

Observations on the Subject of a Note by M. Béchamp, relative to the Nature of the silk-worm Disease.

Observation on the Subject of a Note by M. Béchamp, relative to the Nature of the present silk-worm Disease.

Observation on the Subject of a Note by M. Balbiani, relative to the silk-worm Disease.

New experimental Studies of the silk-worm Disease.

1866 Remarks on the Occasion of a Note by M. Donné regarding spontaneous Generation of infusorial Animalcula.

Observations on the Subject of a Note by M. Pouchet regarding vital Resistance.

1867 Letter to M. Dumas on the Nature of Corpuscles in Silk-worms.

Letter to M. Dumas on the Disease of Silkworms.

1868 Observations relative to Experiments described in a Communication from M.

Chauveau regarding the Nature of vaccine Virus.

Letter addressed to M. Dumas, regarding precocious Cultures of silk-worm eggs of native Stock resulting from selective Breeding.

Letter to M. Dumas on the Subject of the
Disease of Silk-worms.

Second Letter to M. Dumas. Precocious
Cultures of Eggs of native Stock resulting from selective Breeding.

Note on the silk-worm Disease popularly designated by the Name of *morts blancs* or *morts flats*.

Report by M. Pasteur regarding his Commission in 1868 in Relation to the silkworm Disease.

Regarding a Method of determining, through early Experiments on silk-worm Eggs, which of them are predisposed to the Disease of *morts flats*.

1869 Letter addressed to Marechal Vaillant, on the good Effect of cellular Selection in the Culture of silk-worm Eggs.

Letter to M. Dumas, apropos of a letter from M. Cornalia on the proposed Method of regenerating the Breeds of Silk-worms.

Result of Observations made upon the Disease of *morts flats*, both hereditary and accidental.

Observations relating to a previous Communication by M. Raybaud-Lange, on the Disease of *morts flats* and the Method of combatting it. Letter to Marechal Vaillant.

Note on the Selection of Cocoons made by Aid of the Microscope for the Purpose of Regenerating the native Breeds of Silkworms.

Result of two small Cultures of Silk-worms reared from Eggs studied by M. Pasteur.

Note on the Industry of silk-worm Eggs and on the Quality of native Eggs, on the Occasion of a Report of the Silk Commission of Lyons.

Of the Practice of heating, for the Preservation and Amelioration of Wines.

Note on the Subject of a Complaint from M. Paul Thenard, relating to the Heating of Wines.

Note relating to the Communications of M. de Vergnette-Lamotte and M. P. Thenard addressed to the Academy at the Meetings of September 20 and October 4.

Reply to the last Note of M. P. Thenard regarding the Heating of Wines.

1870 Letter to Maréchal Vaillant regarding the Results obtained from the Culture of French Breeds of Silk-worms, effected by means of Eggs obtained by a Process of Selection.

1871 Note on a Memorandum by M. Liebig, relative to fermentation.

Reply to some Remarks by M. Frémy, relative to the preceding Communication.

Observations apropos of a Communication from M. Trécul regarding the Origin of lactic and alcoholic Yeasts.

Concerning the Nature and Origin of Ferments. Reply to a Note inserted by M. Frémy, in the Report of the Meeting of January 15, 1872.

Observations on the Subject of Communications from M. Frémy.

New Observations on the Subject of Communications from M. Frémy.

Observations relative to Communications from M. de Vergnette-Lamotte, on the Preservation of Wines.

Reply to the Communication from M. de Vergnette-Lamotte, concerning the Preservation of Wines,

Concerning the Amelioration of Wines through the Application of Heat.

New Experiments to prove that the Germ of the Yeast which produces Wine comes from the Grapes themselves.

Reply to a Communication by M. Frémy concerning the Generation of Ferments.

New Facts leading to a better Understanding of the Theory of Fermentations properly so called.

Reply of M. Pasteur to M. Frémy.

Observations on the Subject of two Notes which M. Frémy had published in the Report of the Meeting of October 7th.

Reply to a Note by M. Trécul, regarding the Origin of Yeasts.

Note on the Production of Alcohol in Fruit.

Note in Regard to an Assertion by M. Frémy published in the last Report.

Reply to new verbal Observations by M. Frémy. M. Pasteur demands that a Committee be appointed to pass upon the Exactitude of the Experiments mentioned during the Discussion.

Reply to Remarks by M. Trécul, in regard to the Origin of lactic and alcoholic Yeasts.

Observations on the Subject of three Notes communicated by Messrs. Béchamp and Estor at the last Meeting.

1873 Note relating to a Report from M. Cornalier regarding the Culture of Silk-worms during 1872.

A Study of Beer; a new Process to render it unalterable.

Observations in Regard to a Communication from M. Vignon, entitled: "The rotary Power in Mannite."

Reply to a Note on the Origin of Brewer's Yeast, read by M. Trécul at the Meeting of December 8th, 1873.

Reply to M. Trécul regarding the Origin of Brewer's Yeast.

New Reply to M, Trécul regarding the Origin of Brewer's Yeast.

1874 Observations relating to a Communication from Messrs. A. Gosselin and A. Robin, in Regard to ammoniacal Urine.

On the Production of Yeast in a sweetened mineral Medium.

Some Observations in Regard to the natural Dissymmetric Forces.

Observations apropos of a Communication from M. Dumas regarding the Interest that there might be in examining the Effect produced upon Grape

Vines by the Coexistence of Phylloxera and of Mycelium shown to have occurred at Cully.

1875 New Observations upon alcoholic Fermentation.

Concerning a new Distinction between natural organic Products and artificial organic Products.

Observations on the Origin of Sugar in Plants.

Notes on the cellular Method of Cultivating silk-worm Eggs.

Note and Fermentation apropos of some Criticisms made by Doctors Brefeld and Traube.

Concerning the Origin of organic Ferments, apropos of two Communications from M. Frémy and Mr. Tyndall.

1876 Verbal Observations apropos of a Communication from M. Boussingault regarding the Growth and Development of Indian Corn.

Concerning the Fermentation of Urine.

Reply to Observations by M. Berthelot, in Regard to the Theory of Fermentations.

Note on the Subject of a Communication from M. Sace, entitled: Breadmaking in the United States and the Properties of Hops as a Ferment.

Note on the Fermentation of Fruits, and on the Nature of the Germs of alcoholic Yeasts.

Note on the Subject of a Communication made by M. During, regarding the cellulosic Fermentation of Sugar-cane.

1877 Note on the Alteration of Urine, apropos of a Communication from Dr. Bastian, of London.

Reply to a Note from M. Frémy on the ultra-cellular Generation of alcoholic Ferment.

On the Alteration of Urine, apropos of recent Communications from Doctor Bastian.

Verbal Observations on the Occasion of a Communication from M. Bouillant in Regard to typhoid Fever.

Concerning the Fermentation of Urine. Reply to Dr. Bastian.

Reply to Dr. Bastian, regarding Bacteria Germs held in Suspension in the Atmosphere and in Water.

Concerning the Preservation of Food.

Concerning the Fermentation of Urine. Re
ply to Dr. Bastian.

Note on the Subject of a recent Communication from M. Woddell, concerning the Advantages that would result from substituting Cinchonidine for Quinine.

A Study of the Disease of Anthrax.

Remarks on a Communication from M. Raynard.

Note on Anthrax and Septicemia.

Anthrax and Septicemia.

Note on the Subject of Dr. Bastian's Experiment in regard to Urine neutralized by Potash.

1878 Reply to some Remarks by M. Trécul on the Origin of alcoholic Yeasts.

The Theory of Germs and its Application to Medicine and to Surgery.

Observations on the memorandum by Mr. Gunning, entitled: *Concerning Anaërobiosis of Micro-organisms.*

Concerning Anthrax in Poultry, in Collaboration with Messrs. Joubert and Chamberland.

Last Experiments of Claude Bernard. Alcoholic Fermentation. Note on the Theory of Fermentation.

New Communication on the Subject of Notes on alcoholic Fermentation, found among the Papers of Claude Bernard.

Critical Examination of a posthumous Paper by Claude Bernard on alcoholic Fermentation.

Reply to M. Berthelot, relating to alcoholic Fermentation.

Reply to the Observations of M. Trécul relative to Fermentation.

1879 Observations relative to a Note by M. Trécul, on the Subject of lower Organisms.

Second Reply to M. Berthelot.

Reply to Notes by M. Trécul, dated December 30 and January 30.

Observations on the Reply by M. Trécul.

Third Reply to M. Berthelot.

Fermentations. Verbal Observations addressed to M. Trécul.

Fourth Reply to M. Berthelot.

Remarks on the Occasion of a Communication from M. Feltz in Regard to a Leptothrix found in the Blood of a Woman suffering from acute puerperal Fever.

Remarks on the Occasion of a Communication from M. Feltz concerning microscopic Organisms,

Verbal Observations apropos of a Communication from Messrs. Ed. and H. Becquerel, as to the Degree of Cold which may be endured by the Bacteria of Anthrax and by other microscopic Organisms without their losing their Virulence.

1880 Concerning virulent Diseases, and, more particularly, the Disease popularly known as chicken Cholera,

Remarks on the Occasion of a Note from M. Rommier, relating to the toxic Influence which Mycelium in the Roots of the Grape-vine exerts upon Phylloxera.

Reply to M. Blanchard on the Occasion of Observations on a Note by M. Romier concerning the toxic Influence which Mycelium of the Roots of the Grape-vine exerts upon Phylloxera.

Concerning Chicken Cholera; Studies of the Conditions of Non-recurrence of the Disease and certain other Characteristics.

Concerning Chicken Cholera; Studies of the Conditions of Non-recurrence of the Disease and certain other Characteristics.

Concerning the Extension of the Theory of Germs and the Etiology of certain common Maladies.

Concerning the Etiology of Anthrax.

Letter to M. Dumas. Experiments tending to prove that Poultry vaccinated for Chicken Cholera are immune from Anthrax.

Letter to M. Dumas, regarding the Etiology of Diseases of the anthrax Order (in collaboration with M. Chamberland).

Concerning the Attenuation of the Virus of Chicken Cholera.

New Observations on the Etiology and Prophylaxis of Anthrax.

On the Length of Life of the anthrax Germs and their Persistence in cultivated Ground.

Concerning the Attenuation of Viruses and their Return to Virulence.

Regarding the Possibility of rendering Sheep immune from Anthrax by the Method of Preventive Inoculation.

The Vaccine of Anthrax.

Concerning Hydrophobia.

Concerning Vaccination against Anthrax.

Observation apropos of a Note from Messrs.

Arloing, Cornevin and Thomas, regarding the Cause of the Immunity of Adults of the bovine Species from Anthrax.

1882 Concerning *Rouget* or the "red Disease" of Swine.

New Facts helpful to an Understanding of Hydrophobia.

Statistics on the Subject of Vaccination as a Preventive against Anthrax, based upon eighty-five thousand Animals.

1883 Concerning Vaccination against Anthrax.

The veterinary Commission of Turin.

Telegraphic Despatch addressed to M. Dumas.

Vaccination of Swine against *Rouget* by Means of an Attenuation of the deadly Virus of that Disease.

1884 New Communication in regard to Hydrophobia.

Concerning Hydrophobia.

Observations in Regard to a Note by M. Duclaux, relating to Germination in a Soil rich in organic Matter but exempt from Microbes.

Method for preventing Hydrophobia after the Patient has been bitten.

Reply to Remarks by Messrs. Vulpian, Bouley and Larrey.

1886 Results of the Application of the Method of preventing Hydrophobia after the Patient has been bitten.

Reply to Observations by the President and by M. Vulpian apropos of the preceding Communication.

Supplementary Note on the Results of the Application of the Method of Prophylaxis of Hydrophobia after having been bitten.

Observations relating to a Communication by M. Picetti regarding a new Species of Asparagine.

New communication regarding Hydrophobia.

1887 Statistical Summary of the Persons who have been treated at the Pasteur Institute after having been bitten by Animals that either had hydrophobia or were suspected of having it.

Note accompanying the Presentation of the

Report of the English Commission on Hydrophobia.

1888 Concerning the first Volume of Annals of the

Pasteur Institute, and more particularly a Memorandum by Messrs. Roux and Chamberland, entitled: *Immunity from Septicemia, conferred by soluble Substances.*

Remarks relating to a Communication from M. Gamaleia concerning preventive Vaccination against Asiatic Cholera.

1889 Concerning the Method of Prophylaxis of Hydrophobia after the Patient has been bitten.

Printed in the USA
CPSIA information can be obtained
at www.ICGtesting.com
LVHW041244051023
760079LV00002B/637